Spirit of the North

Spirit of the North

THE QUOTABLE SIGURD F. OLSON

Sigurd F. Olson
Edited by David Backes

UNIVERSITY OF MINNESOTA PRESS
MINNEAPOLIS • LONDON

Published by the University of Minnesota Press
111 Third Avenue South, Suite 290
Minneapolis, MN 55401-2520
http://www.upress.umn.edu

Printed in the United States of America on acid-free paper

Library of Congress Cataloging-in-Publication Data

Olson, Sigurd F., 1899–1982
   Spirit of the North : the quotable Sigurd F. Olson / Sigurd F. Olson ; edited by David Backes.
      p. cm.
Includes bibliographical references (p.   ).
   ISBN 0-8166-3934-5 (HC : alk. paper)
  1. Olson, Sigurd F., 1899–1982—Quotations. 2. Natural history.
3. Natural history—Minnesota. I. Backes, David. II. Title.
QH31.O47 A3   2004
508.776—dc22

                                    2003014896

12 11 10 09 08 07 06 05 04   10 9 8 7 6 5 4 3 2 1

To Bob, Vonnie, and Sig Jr.

To see a World in a grain of sand,
        And a Heaven in a wild flower
Hold Infinity in the palm of your hand,
        And Eternity in an hour.

—WILLIAM BLAKE

Contents

Preface

In *Reflections from the North Country*, Sigurd Olson spoke of his lifelong admiration for Robert Service, the bard of frontier Alaska. Service wrote poems, such as "The Cremation of Sam McGee," that even a century later are read to schoolchildren. He loved to recite Service's poems and in his writings occasionally quoted parts of them, such as these lines from the end of "The Call of the Wild":

> There's a whisper in the night-wind, there's a star agleam to
> guide us,
> And the Wild is calling, calling—let us go.

"Somehow in his poems," Olson wrote in *Reflections from the North Country*, "he caught the spirit of the North, the cold, suffering, and hardship in pursuit of some bonanza. . . . Some call them crude unlettered doggerel and perhaps they are right, but he touches the hearts of men and for that he will live on as long as Alaskan wilderness remains."

Ever since I first began my research for Olson's biography more than a dozen years ago, I have run into many people who quote from his writings the way he quoted from Service's poems. There are many favorites: "The movement of a canoe is like a reed in the wind"; "Over all was the silence of the wilderness, that sense of oneness which comes only when there are no distracting sights or sounds, when we listen with inward ears and see with inward eyes"; "Every bit of water had turned to gold and, as the valley darkened, it looked as if molten metal had been spilled and dribbled over the black velvet of the land." Some people especially like his descriptions of nature, others recall his most philosophical musings, and still others recite lines about camping, canoeing, or fishing. All would say about Olson what he said about Service: "he left a feeling for the land and captured its lure as no other man has ever done."

Olson did more than *capture* the spirit: to many he *is* the spirit of the North, especially the more accessible North of the Quetico–Superior canoe country of northern Minnesota and Ontario. He was the most beloved wilderness advocate of his generation, and his name and image evoked strong feelings. Often photographed with a pipe in his hand and a warm yet reflective expression on his weathered face, he was a hero—an icon—of the wilderness preservation movement. His books were read on public radio, his portrait was taken by Alfred Eisenstaedt for *Life* magazine, and awards almost routinely came his way. Today, more than twenty years after his death, the popularity of his biography and the continuing sales of his writings indicate a persistent interest in Olson and a new generation reading his works and being drawn to the North as countless others have been.

Excerpts from some of his best nature writing and key statements of his wilderness philosophy give both the newcomer and the longtime fan a good sense of Olson the man. The quotations come from his books and magazine articles and from his journals, letters, and speeches as well. I hope to do more than simply provide passages that are memorable for their prose or for their philosophical power; I want to give a sense of

his development over time as a person, a writer, a conservationist, and a wilderness philosopher. Each chapter
focuses on a fundamental aspect of his life or beliefs.
Most chapters have several categories that relate to the
overall topic, and quotations are arranged chronologi-
cally within each category to show the evolution of his
thought over time. Several quotations, of course, are
appropriate for more than one category or chapter; I
simply placed these where I thought they would do the
most good. If I have chosen well, perhaps you will understand why I, like many others, could take his words
about Service, change them just a little, and apply them
to Olson himself: he touches our hearts and for that he
will live on as long as wilderness remains.

Acknowledgments

I am deeply grateful once again to Todd Orjala, Pieter Martin, and the rest of the wonderful people at the University of Minnesota Press. I greatly appreciate the kindness you have shown me and the care you have given to my books over the years. Thank you!

My wife, Judi, and Heidi, Tim, Jenny, and Andrew have given me much love and support, and also have helped me regain perspective when I become obsessed with deadlines and the other pressures of writing. I am happy that they know the value of helping to support the dreams of others and the importance of following their own as well. That, in the end, is the most important lesson I have learned from Sigurd Olson—follow your heart, not only for your sake but for the sake of others.

To Bob, Vonnie, and Sig Jr.: words cannot express how happy I am that you entered my life all those years ago. The welcome you gave me right from the very beginning—back when you knew I was going to write about your father and father-in-law and had no idea whether or not that would be a good thing—was amazing. Now we are simply family, and my heart is full, and I will always be grateful for the love we share. This book, most of all, is for you.

Chronology of Sigurd Olson's Life

1899	Born in Humboldt Park, Chicago, on April 4.
1906	Family moves to Sister Bay, Wisconsin, on the rugged Door County Peninsula.
1909	Family moves to Prentice, a logging town in north central Wisconsin.
1912	Family moves to Ashland, Wisconsin, on the edge of Lake Superior.
1916–18	Sigurd attends Northland College in Ashland; works during the summers at a farm in Seeley, Wisconsin, owned by Soren Uhrenholdt.
1918–20	Sigurd attends the University of Wisconsin in Madison; earns an undergraduate degree in agriculture.
1920–22	Sigurd teaches animal husbandry, agricultural botany, and geology in the high schools of the neighboring northern Minnesota towns of Nashwauk and Keewatin.
1921	Sigurd takes his first canoe trip in June; marries Elizabeth Dorothy Uhrenholdt on August 8. Their honeymoon is a three-week canoe trip. Eight days before the wedding, on July 31, the *Milwaukee Journal* publishes Sigurd's first article, an account of his June canoe trip.
1922	Sigurd starts in a graduate program in geology at the University of Wisconsin in Madison; Elizabeth helps with finances by teaching elementary school in Hayward, Wisconsin.
1923	In January Elizabeth learns she is pregnant. Sigurd drops out of school and lands a job teaching high school biology in Ely, Minnesota,

at the edge of the canoe country wilderness. They move there in February. During the summer, Sigurd works as a canoe trip guide, which he continues to do every summer throughout the 1920s. Sigurd and Elizabeth become parents on September 15, when Sigurd Thorne Olson is born.

1925   Robert Keith Olson is born on December 23. Sigurd is involved in the first battle over the canoe country wilderness, a conflict about proposals to build roads into previously inaccessible areas.

1926   In September, the U.S. Secretary of Agriculture ends the current canoe country conflict by allowing two major roads to be built and by creating three wilderness areas within Superior National Forest. Sigurd begins splitting his teaching duties between Ely High School and Ely Junior College. At the junior college, he teaches animal biology and human physiology.

1927   In November *Field and Stream* publishes Sigurd's first magazine article, "Fishin' Jewelry."

1929   Sigurd and two other men found the Border Lakes Outfitting Company. As manager, Sigurd spends less time guiding. He manages the company until the mid-1940s and maintains partial ownership until 1951.

1931–32   In the fall of 1931, the Olsons move to Champaign, Illinois, so Sigurd can earn a master's degree in zoology at the University of Illinois. Sigurd works under Victor Shelford, the nation's leading animal ecologist. He earns his degree in June 1932 after completing a thesis—the first of its kind—on the timber wolf. The Olsons move back to Ely, and Sigurd begins teaching full-time at Ely Junior College.

1932   In May and June, *Sports Afield* publishes Sigurd's two-part article "Search for the Wild," his first article fully devoted to wilderness philosophy.

1936	Sigurd becomes dean of Ely Junior College.
1938	In September *American Forests* publishes Sigurd's article "Why Wilderness?" Superior National Forest's three wilderness areas, recently enlarged, are renamed the Superior Roadless Areas.
1941	Sigurd begins a syndicated newspaper column, "America Out of Doors." It lasts until 1944, when (like many syndicated columns of the time) it dies as government wartime restrictions on newsprint force newspapers to cut back.
1945	In June, Sigurd heads to Europe for a year as a civilian employee of the army. He teaches GIs waiting to be shipped back to America and is an official observer at the Nuremburg trials.
1947	Sigurd resigns as dean of Ely Junior College to devote full time to his writing.
1948–49	Sigurd spearheads the fight to ban airplanes from the wilderness canoe country near his home. It is a precedent-setting, successful battle and brings Sigurd national recognition in conservation circles.
1951	Sigurd becomes vice president of the National Parks Association.
1953	Sigurd becomes president of the National Parks Association.
1955	The year begins with Sigurd signing his first book contract, with Alfred A. Knopf. In the summer, Sigurd and a group of prominent Canadian friends spend several weeks paddling the wild Churchill River in Saskatchewan, one of a handful of rugged trips they would take together.
1956	*The Singing Wilderness* is published in April, shortly after Sigurd's fifty-seventh birthday. It becomes a *New York Times* best-seller. In the summer, the Wilderness Society elects Sigurd to its governing council. Sigurd is among the conservation leaders working on

drafts of a bill to establish a national wilderness preservation system.

1958   *Listening Point* is published. The Superior Roadless Areas are renamed the Boundary Waters Canoe Area.

1959   Sigurd resigns as president of the National Parks Association and joins the advisory board of the National Park Service. He remains on the board until 1966.

1961   *The Lonely Land* is published.

1962   Sigurd becomes a consultant on wilderness and national park matters for Secretary of the Interior Stewart Udall.

1963   *Runes of the North* is published. Sigurd becomes vice president of the Wilderness Society.

1964   In July, sixty-five-year-old Sigurd embarks on his last major canoe expedition, a voyage from Lake Winnipeg to Hudson Bay along the Nelson and Hayes Rivers. In September, President Lyndon B. Johnson signs the Wilderness Act, establishing the national wilderness preservation system.

1965   Sigurd is part of a National Park Service task force that recommends preserving nearly eighty million acres of land in Alaska. Fearing a political firestorm, the agency buries the report, but the work behind it ultimately bears fruit in the Alaska National Interest Lands and Conservation Act of 1980.

1968   Sigurd becomes president of the Wilderness Society. In November, he suffers a major heart attack during the society's annual meeting at Sanibel Island, Florida.

1969   *Open Horizons* and *The Hidden Forest* are published.

1971   Sigurd resigns as president of the Wilderness Society, citing his health and desire to write. President Nixon signs into law the act establishing Voyageurs National Park in northern Minnesota; Sigurd had played an important role as an advocate of the park since the early 1960s, and he also gave the park its name. A new elementary school in the Minneapolis suburb of Golden Valley is named after Sigurd.

1972   *Wilderness Days* is published. The Sigurd Olson Environmental Institute is established at Northland College in Ashland, Wisconsin.

1974   The highest honor in nature writing, the John Burroughs Medal, is presented to Sigurd.

1976   *Reflections from the North Country* is published.

1977   Sigurd is hanged in effigy in his hometown of Ely, Minnesota, during debates about the status of the Boundary Waters Canoe Area.

1978   President Jimmy Carter signs the law granting full wilderness status to the Boundary Waters Canoe Area Wilderness, more than fifty years after Sigurd's first efforts to protect it.

1979   In December, Sigurd undergoes successful surgery for colon cancer. He never fully regains his strength.

1982   On January 13, Sigurd dies of a heart attack while snowshoeing near his home. *Of Time and Place* is published.

1994   Elizabeth Olson dies of heart failure on August 23 at the age of ninety-six.

1998   The Listening Point Foundation is established to preserve and protect Listening Point, the northern Minnesota lakeshore property that served as a getaway place for Sigurd, and to promote his philosophy and build on his legacy in the field of wilderness education.

THE SEARCH

Reading Sigurd Olson's books and looking at the dust jacket photos, it is easy to imagine him as he often was portrayed by devoted followers in the 1960s and 1970s: the optimistic, wise icon of wilderness peace. One would never guess that he had gone through a sometimes agonizing search for meaning and fulfillment. From the 1920s through the 1940s, he strongly identified with Henry David Thoreau's statement that "most men lead lives of quiet desperation." He felt stifled as a high school teacher and later junior college professor and dean, tried a master's degree program in geology only to drop out, and earned a master's degree in ecology only to decide he hated scientific research. His deepest happiness came from spending as much time as possible exploring the lakes, rivers, and woods of his beloved canoe country, and from putting his experiences on paper and trying to convey to others the spiritual benefits of nature. He dreamed of being able to quit teaching and devote full time to writing, but for many years received far more rejections—often accompanied by scathing criticism—than he did encouragement. His journals of the 1930s and 1940s are full of pain, and while some of the excerpts printed here indicate an egotistical sense of his ability and importance, in fact he often came close to giving up. Not until 1956, at the age of fifty-seven, when Alfred Knopf published *The Singing Wilderness* and it quickly

established itself as a best-seller, did he truly find fulfillment and the peace that came with it.

The first section contains some general quotations
about Olson's search for meaning, purpose, and direction. This is followed by statements showing his deep
passion for the outdoors and his experiences as a canoe
country guide. The final sections explore his thoughts
about three career tracks: the possibility of becoming a
scientist, his actual career for many years as a classroom
teacher, and his dream and true vocation of teaching
through writing.

On Following a Dream

Think of the wonder of being able to live on dreams, of
being able to do what more than all else in the world
you have wanted to do. Think of the wonder of knowing
that you have found yourself.

– Journal, January 14, 1930

Many go through life without making an effort to
unearth the hidden stores within them and die having
lived sterile lives in their own arid deserts. Many go
through stifled by the narrowness of their daily affairs
little dreaming that at their very doors for the asking
is a wilderness to explore, the wilderness of their
understanding.

– Journal, January 17, 1930

It seems that I do not know what I want, that no matter
where I am, I am unhappy and discontented.

– Journal, September 16, 1932

I feel so strongly sometimes that I know I cannot go on
without satisfying. The emotion I know at times hurts

me terribly. It is all that is worthwhile in life to me. Human feelings—emotions—the only worthwhile things in life. Nothing else matters, just that—love—understanding—sympathy. They are all that is worthwhile—one who can understand and feel must give without stint.

– Journal, ca 1930s

I long to find a sphere in which I can absolutely sink all of my energies, tire myself out, use every iota of nervous energy I possess, lose myself body and soul in whatever I do, wear myself down to bone and raw nerve for such is my nature and such is my intensity. I have reached the stage where the commonplace will not satisfy, where it becomes imperative that I go the limit. I should regret every moment taken away from my work, be so anxious to accomplish what I have set for myself that exhausting labor will be my joy. Only then will I be happy and content.

– Journal, October 21, 1934

All of my life I have searched and found little reality—why I do not know. What is real—what is synthetic . . . I am continually feeling that what I am doing has no basis, no solidity—that I am on the bench watching a show but not a part of it, that I am perched as it were on a limb ready to fly; that there is no permanence—no foundation.

– Journal, February 15, 1939

The frustrations of being tied to schedules and laboratories and lecture rooms so many years gave me a powerful need: I had to write, I had to work my way out, I had to accomplish the impossible. . . . Without the frustration and this resolve I might not have been driven to the point where something had to give. . . . One must have frustrations to build upon. I had them. They matured into the kind of life I am living now.

– Journal, March 29, 1966

Passion for the Outdoors

I have stood on top of a windswept hill, waved my hat at the breeze, shouted to the skies that I was alive, and I have fought the waves on gigantic lakes and enjoyed the slap of every one. I love the rain, the snow, thunder, storms, quiet, every change of the weather.

– Journal, March 4, 1935

This morning, not able to stand it a moment longer, I started out over the old hills I know so well. . . . It was balm to my shattered nerves and it did me good. How wonderful it was lying under that big spruce to hear the spring song of the first robins. . . . I tried to think out my problem but all I could think of was the beauty of the sunlight, the sound of the wind through my spruce and the silhouette of the birches over the hill to the west. The more I tried to think the more soothing grew the influences around me. . . . How true that has been all the time. Great thoughts do not come to me when I am out. . . . When I am out I am too receptive, too liable to see only and feel, I become entirely sensuous, an animal soaking up the impressions of color, and light and smell and sound.

– Journal, April 9, 1935

As long as I can remember I have felt I must get out in the sunshine, must feel the wind or the rain in my face,

must have open sky and open visions all around.
I cannot stand to be inside for very long especially
when the weather is good.

– Journal, March 30, 1966

One of the great frustrations in school was to have to
stay in and close my eyes to the out of doors. So
powerful was this urge that when Friday came I just
had to take off, it did not matter where.

– Journal, March 30, 1966

I do not think the time will ever come when I could be
resigned to being inside.

– Journal, March 30, 1966

I was jealous of every moment I spent indoors. I hated
to miss a sunset or a sunrise, hated to miss the feel of
wind on my face or the rain. It was not long before I
developed a reputation as a sort of crackpot, but there
it was.

– "The Long Long Dances" (draft of *Open Horizons* chapter),
April 4, 1966

Nobody in the family understood why on earth I had to
be running off in the woods all the time. I'd take off for
the boondocks and be gone all day.

– Quoted in Jim Dale Vickery, "The Legacy of Sig Olson,"
Boundary Waters Journal, Winter 1988

Guiding

On my canoe trips, much to the secret amusement of
my parties, I used to steal away for a silent paddle by
myself after the others had gone to bed. They used to

chide me about my peculiarities in the morning and make inferences as to my poetic leanings. Many of them would understand, however, and I would detect a feeling of understanding and sympathy.

– Journal, January 20, 1930

As the guiding went on, first friendships ripened into loyalties and when old parties returned the trips were always happy reunions. Now when we meet after many years there is still a common bond that over-rides the divergence of our trails. . . . Why such casual contacts in the bush should have ripened into firm friendships among men with little common background is due I believe to the fact that in the bush old reserves and inhibitions become meaningless and men know each other for exactly what they are. In all the men I came to know there is the hope that in a world of tension, strife and change that somehow there will always be places to travel where they can recapture the laughter and the fun they once knew.

– "Something Lost beyond the Ranges" (draft of *Open Horizons* chapter), November 17, 1966

I felt that only by knowing the men who made their living there could I ever really understand and catch the full flavor and meaning of the land itself. . . . I wanted more than the actual guiding; I needed to know these guides and their feelings about the country they had explored, what motivated them and why they lived as they did.

– *Open Horizons,* 82, 85

Each one had developed certain skills, the result of many years of living in the woods. None could explain how or when he had acquired them, but whatever its explanation, it worked, and even as I did, they watched each other until inevitably a guide was a broad composite of the total experience of every man he had been with.

– *Open Horizons*, 97

But there was something more I got from them—their feeling for the land itself. This I have never forgotten, and when cities bear too heavily, I remember the guides of the Quetico–Superior who had no subtleties or hidden purposes, to whom the idea of contracts and influence was foreign, and who were as genuine and down to earth as the rocky shores of the waterways they followed.

– *Open Horizons*, 98–99

To be sure, I had known [silence] in the past, but not in the way I knew it as a guide, the cumulative effect of days and weeks on end. This was more than temporary release from noise, it was a primordial thing that seeped into the deepest recesses of the mind until mechanical intrusions were intolerable.

– *Open Horizons*, 102

Science

How many scientists are cold analysts, how many of them lose sight of the wonder of creation. How often do they fail to see the primary underlying principle of existence. How often do they fail to see the beauty thru their microscope and statistical intelligence. To me beauty is all, to me it is far more worthwhile to feel the glory of a sunny morning on the snow than it is to obtain a new specimen.

– Journal, January 12, 1930

As the years roll by I am also convinced that only one happiness is for me and that [is] the steady observance and interpretation of nature and man's relation to it and not scientific research fascinating as that may seem. That does not interest me, perhaps because I do not know enough about it, but I do not think that is it. I know enough from close contact with science to know that it would pall me. I am not interested in seeing a dead mouse or a fine wolf skin. I am interested in knowing how life is lived, how it compares with ours in aim and substance, in interpreting the primitive urge of all breathing things and in studying the beauty or organization rather than the detailed intricacies of analyses and classification.

– Journal, January 16, 1930

I do not want to meddle with too much of science at the sacrifice of my soul. I must retain my original freshness of perception.

– Journal, April 7, 1930

I hate the very sound of the word Ecology, plant or animal. There is something stifling about it that will never quite make it possible for me to go ahead.

– Journal, December 14, 1931

I am beginning to see after all what my main interest in the out of doors has been. It is not a scientific interest as I thought for so many years and still thought until this year. What has kept me in the woods all of these years is the love of beauty. . . . If I was watching a beaver it was

not the beaver and its habits as much as it was the light
on the pool, the dark mystery of the forest around the
pool, the symmetry of the dam. If I was trailing a deer,
it was not so much the habits of the deer as it was the
vistas I gained along the ridges and through the trees.
If it was ducks, it was more than anything else the
view of a flock against the sunset or dawn in the rice
rather than the birds themselves. In other words it was
the scene as a whole which drew me and that I
mistook for a keen interest in natural history for lack
of a better explanation. . . . A job on a university staff
would kill me as would also any job at a wildlife
research station. . . . What I would be doing all of the
time would be longing to paint either in word or color
the pictures that have been before me.

– Journal, December 31, 1931

The secret of my discontent with all scientific research
is that at heart I am not a scientist, although I am rated
as one. I am not interested in any work that has a purely
scientific trend. It bores me to death and always will.
The only thing that will ever give me a thrill is to depict
the emotions that men have, their loves and hates.

– Journal, December 12, 1933

I tried hard to think of biological ideas, mice and
wolves, and plants and all the rest, but they seemed
prosaic to me. I was out to catch something different,
something deeper, the meaning behind all of life.
I pictured myself in New Hampshire, roaming around,
making observations, statistics, helpers, 30 to 40 of
them making observations for me. What do I know
about game management, what do I know or care.

– Journal, April 9, 1935

Teaching

The summer is over and once again I am back at the old grind.

– Journal, September 28, 1930

I must make the break soon. This is not my field, I know it and feel it. Do I wake up in the morning anxious to get at my task, no, I count the hours until the end of the week. Surely no future in that.

– Journal, September 22, 1932

If I can teach the mystery of life and see the joy that such knowledge can give, then I will have done something wonderful. I can live a life of gentleness and understanding and above all get away from the old cut and dried idea that teaching is drudgery. It is really a luxury to be in a position to make such contacts. It is perhaps the noblest of all professions.

– Journal, ca early 1930s

As long as I have to face another winter of teaching and forget the writing I must do, then I will be in agony.

– Journal, August 14, 1934

I enjoy my teaching a great deal, now that it is all Junior College. It is not half bad and the kids love me.

– Journal, September 4, 1934

As I take over a zoology class, I realize that it is all over, that I can never do much in the way of teaching because I know nothing about my subject and am not particularly interested. Look at the exhibit material, the collections, the paucity of stuff, after twenty years in

the department. That is due to lack of enthusiasm and
the pigeonholing of my interest in other channels.

– Journal, May 1, 1940

Spring days when the first flowers were popping
[meant] field trips of identification, hundreds of them,
I could barely wait, and I am afraid I wore out my
students so insistent was I that they feel what I felt.

– "The Long Long Dances" (draft of *Open Horizons* chapter),
April 4, 1966

There must above all be joy and excitement in
learning, and I became convinced that field trips and
observations were as important as books and
laboratories.

– "Home from the Hill" (draft of *Open Horizons* chapter),
April 3, 1967

What I brought back from my own expeditions was an
evolving, fresher point of view that colored and
breathed life into factual information that had grown
dusty away from sunlight and open air. By returning to
the source of all knowledge, nature itself, the power of
wonder could play its part.

– "Home from the Hill" (draft of *Open Horizons* chapter),
April 3, 1967

During that first fall, I practically deserted the
classroom, discovered anew the tremendous value of
field observation no matter what the general course
work involved. Slides, dissections, and books were vital,
but only in reference to the living world; better to know
a bird, flower, or a rock in its natural setting than to rely
solely on routine identification and description. This
kind of teaching had as much to do with awareness and

appreciation as the actual accumulation of knowledge. Observations on the ground, I decided, were just as important as laboratory experiments; in fact, they went hand in hand, and one without the other was meaningless to me.

– *Open Horizons*, 69

Writing

Your greatest happiness is to express yourself, see yourself in print. If you could make enough money writing so that you wouldn't have to teach, and would have enough time to roam around, I really think you could be reasonably happy.

– Journal, January 15, 1930

I am not happiest when I am writing but I am perhaps happiest just after I am through. It is like physical pain, really enjoyable in a sense because of the relief after it is over, so with writing, not so pleasant at the time, although one must admit that there is some pleasure to putting down thoughts on paper, but satisfaction afterward that counts most.

– Journal, January 16, 1930

There are few who see what I see, very few. Even the great writers of nature, many of them have failed. Occasionally there crops out an inkling of it but none of the clearness of perception and depth of feeling that I know. Why I should have it I cannot know, perhaps it is an inherited instinct from some far ancestral mystic. Surely none of my family [has] it, if they do it is hidden and unrecognizable. In me have been concentrated the natural mysticism of centuries of my race. I have been given the seeing eye. It is my mission to give my vision to the race in return for the beauty that has been shown me. I cannot go through life keeping it to myself. That would be rank ingratitude to the nature I worship.

– Journal, January 20, 1930

If my outfitting business would only get sufficiently on its feet so that I could devote six months of the year to writing at my own pace and speed, I really think I would accomplish something worthwhile.

– Journal, January 22, 1930

I must have freedom above all else and writing is the only occupation that will give it to me.

– Journal, January 22, 1930

I must write. I cannot live and not write.

– Journal, April 2, 1930

Putting in my worst hours on what I love most, stealing time from my work to do what means most is atrophying to say the least. . . . I am as I am for a purpose. . . . The popular nature writers have never touched the depths whatever. Theirs have been mere frothy descriptions of what they have seen and experienced but they have never given people what they want. That is my task. A new type of story with a touch of the spiritual in it, a deeper understanding and appreciation. . . . I have faith in myself, a faith that I have what others have not. In that egotism lies my greatest strength.

– Journal, April 7, 1930

These days have been days of darkness to me, days of indecision and doubt when I haven't known for the life of me whether I was going to continue with my writing or go into scientific research. It is queer but the very instant that I decide to give up my writing and go into science I become miserable.

– Journal, December 4, 1930

No one has as yet developed a philosophy of the wilderness. That is up to me. . . . My work must be strong and hard and masculine, the love of men for the wild, its truth, its unvarnished joy, its compensations, the feeling of being alone.

– Journal, November 21, 1934

It will not make much difference if I don't write anything worthwhile from a financial standpoint. I must write to keep my sanity. Writing is the insulin of a disease of long standing. I must take my regular dose or go under.

– Journal, ca mid-1930s

Black and white is my canvas, words my pigments, interpretation of the wild my theme.

– Journal, January 14, 1937

By the looks of things, the world will not discover me until I am dead. Perhaps the world is better off at that.

– Letter to Don Hough, March 3, 1939

Last night was typical, so is every gathering. I go with the rest, laugh and joke and supposedly have a good time, but underneath it all, I feel that I should not be wasting my time, that I should be away somewhere writing. Writing, writing—it never leaves me. The

duck hunting coming up will be the same. I will finally
manage to get the gang to Basswood and while there
will try and get enthusiastic, will try and lose myself as
Wilson, and Ray, and Alec and Junior do, but it will be
the same. It has been the same for years. I can never
forget, can never get over the idea that I am marking
time, am part of shadow America.

– Journal, September 22, 1939

The only part of writing that I really like is the first draft
where you are really getting your ideas down. After
that the endless polishing and revision is just plain
backbreaking work. Occasionally when a new idea slips
through, it is fun again, but mostly just work. However,
be that as it may, a session like last night always leaves
me feeling good and enthusiastic which is more than
I can say for anything else I might be doing.

– Journal, December 13, 1939

I do not wish to entertain, I want to write deeply, I want
to wring from my innermost soul the thoughts that lie
there fallow and waiting.

– Journal, April 9, 1940

I am a harp on whose sensitive strings the winds of
the world blow and my task is to set to music the
strains I alone can hear.

– Journal, May 2, 1940

I feel that I have a message to contribute, something real
and vital that many are missing. If I can make them feel
about the woods and hills and waters as I do, about
every little thing that gives me pleasure, then I have
done enough. There is something of the crusader in me,
the evangelist. I cannot rest unless it comes out and I

will never be happy unless I give myself wholly to the task at hand.

– Journal, ca 1942–1943

The only reason you want to write is to tell your story
1. Make men feel close to nature and joy
2. Show that God is love
3. Show that God is spirit
4. That the primitive is past, that man is now a spiritual animal. Nature is cruel—implacable—harsh—Man thru his insight changes things.

– Journal, ca January 1950

The things I write about, homely simple episodes of life here in the Quetico–Superior, or gleaned from my roamings all over the north, will have as their basic purpose bridging the gap between our absorption with modern science and a growing materialism and a new humanism that will somehow give the reader something to hold on to, an understanding of our place in an expanding universe where we are swiftly finding out all of the answers. If I can contribute even in a small way to stilling some of the hunger and groping and confusion which besets us all, then even the effort is worthwhile.

– Letter to Angus Cameron, February 16, 1961

You separate yourself from your family, from your friends, from your social obligations—it's between you and the page.

– In *The Wilderness World of Sigurd F. Olson,* Twin Cities Public Television, 1980

You've got to want very much to write. Writing must become the most important thing in the world to you. . . . I felt I must write, I must keep at it, I must forget my rejection slips, of which I had millions. You've got to want to write badly enough to keep on in spite of anything else. And even at the tender age of eighty, my greatest happiness is sitting down and working on this next book.

– In *The Wilderness World of Sigurd F. Olson*, Twin Cities Public Television, 1980

A STRANGE AND VIOLENT WORLD

Sigurd Olson believed Americans put far too much faith in technology, materialism, and a scientific perspective in which the only truths are those that can be measured and quantified. Underneath the nation's growing wealth lies an inner poverty and restless longing that cannot be addressed without a fundamental change of perspective that recognizes the limits of science and of material progress as well as the spiritual truths that are essential for a sense of meaning and obvious to those who slow down enough to look and listen. The quotations in this chapter examine various aspects of Olson's critique of society.

It is slowly dawning upon us that the solution of the world's problems are to be found in the fields of social attitudes, human values, the spiritual fields of ideals, character, and culture, and not in the immediately practical considerations of scientific progress.

– Untitled speech for a Legion Auxiliary memorial service, Ely, Minnesota, May 1, 1940

City life is artificial. Because artificiality leads to a sense of unreality and frustration, unhappiness often results. That is the price a people pays for high technological success, and that is the reason an intelligent, thinking people knows that unless it can break away and renew its contact with a slow-moving natural philosophy, it will lose its perspective and forget simplicity and wholesomeness.

> – "We Need Wilderness," *National Parks Magazine,*
> January–March 1946

Because of our almost forgotten past there is a restlessness within us, an impatience with things as they are, which modern life with its comforts and distractions does not seem to satisfy. We sense intuitively that there must be something more, search for panaceas we hope will give us a sense of reality, fill our days and nights with such activity and our minds with such busyness that there is little time to think. When the pace stops we are often lost, and we plunge once more into the maelstrom hoping that if we move fast enough, somehow we may fill the void within us.

> – *The Singing Wilderness,* 6–7

Civilization has robbed us of much of our sensitivity to smells, has dulled our original powers of perception by too much living indoors. It has substituted the by-products of industrial combustion for the natural smells of earth and water and growing things. Primitive tribes still have the faculty of smelling the weather, but few urban dwellers can sniff the air and tell what kind of day it is going to be, let alone know what flowers are in bloom or what life may be near. Through degeneration of our sense of smell, we only partially enjoy the out-of-doors.

> – *The Singing Wilderness,* 57

Urbanization in its present form is a threat not only to our economy but to our physical and spiritual welfare.

– "Our Need of Breathing Space," in *Perspectives on Conservation*, 1958

Urban man has thrown plans to the winds and is living a catch-as-catch-can existence dominated by impermanence, speed, and fluidity of movement. He is divorcing himself from the earth, and in this divorcement he is losing contact with elemental and spiritual things, his sense of oneness with his environment, psychological and physiological needs for which he has been conditioned for a million years by an entirely different existence.

– "Our Need of Breathing Space," in *Perspectives on Conservation*, 1958

While we may well be able to provide synthetics in fuel, food, and materials to take the place of exhausted resources of the past, cope with an expanding population without starvation or want, the great question will always be: Is this enough, is this the kind of a world we really want to live in?

– "Our Need of Breathing Space," in *Perspectives on Conservation*, 1958

It is wonderful to have national parks and forests to go to, but they are not enough. It is not enough to make a trip once a year or to see these places occasionally over a long week-end. We need to have places close at hand, breathing spaces in cities and towns, little plots of ground where things have not changed; green belts, oases among the piles of steel and stone.

– "Our Need of Breathing Space," in *Perspectives on Conservation*, 1958

While we are born with curiosity and wonder and our early years full of the adventure they bring, I know that such inherent joys are often lost. I also know that, being deep within us, their latent glow can be fanned to flame again by awareness and an open mind.

– *Listening Point*, 4

We are adopting a mechanistic attitude toward life in which we believe science has all the answers, and are abandoning the ancient verities and an appreciation of intangible values. We are confusing mores with morals.

– "The Spiritual Aspects of Wilderness," at Seventh Biennial Wilderness Conference, San Francisco, April 1961

A strange and violent world is ours, with the great silences replaced by the roar of jets and the cities we have built vibrating with noise.

– "The Spiritual Aspects of Wilderness," at Seventh Biennial Wilderness Conference, San Francisco, April 1961

We are trying to bridge the gap between our old racial wisdom, our old primeval consciousness, the old verities, and the strange, conflicting ideologies and beliefs of the new era of technology. One of the most vital tasks of modern man is to bridge this gap. . . . None of us is naive enough to want to give up what technology has brought or to evade the challenges now before us. This too is a frontier, not only of the mind but of the physical world. Somehow we must make the adjustment and bring both ways of life together. If man can do this, if he can span past and present, then he can face the future with confidence.

– "The Spiritual Aspects of Wilderness," at Seventh Biennial Wilderness Conference, San Francisco, April 1961

If we should lose the very desire for those values that are inherent in wilderness and abandon ourselves to the mechanical robot age of automation, then the holocaust of atomic war might be the end of the long dreams of man and his endless search for beauty and meaning in the universe.

– "The Wilderness Concept," *Ames Forester,* 1962 annual

We have forgotten the use of axes and saws, forgotten the joy of doing physical work. How few today know the feel of an axe as it bites into a log, the solid feel of it going into resin, the clean break of a chunk splitting in the cold.

– *Runes of the North,* 70

Ours is a strange and dramatic age, the great silences replaced by the roar of engines, the cities vibrating with noise and foul with gases and pollution. The smells of woods, fields, and forests are replaced by those of combustion and industry, and our senses are bombarded with impressions man has never known before. Were it not for a racial consciousness steeped in a background that knew nothing of technology, we might make the adjustment more easily, but physiological and psychological adaptations take eons of time. Too close to our past to ignore these ancient ties to the earth, and in spite of comforts and luxuries never known before, we are conscious of tensions and a sense of instability.

– *Open Horizons,* 215

In the last few decades we have almost succeeded in weaning ourselves from the past, but in spite of our urbanity, we have not been able to sever our spiritual roots, and I believe this to be the cause of our discontent. With growing divorcement from nature, the change is coming more and more swiftly, and we are now embarking on the greatest adventure and possible tragedy of all, exploring the universe while holding in our hands forces which threaten our survival.

– *Open Horizons*, 216

Many refuse to believe resources are exhaustible and pioneering a thing of the past; inherently we are still part of the boom days with development of the wilds the natural course of events. Talk of intangible and spiritual values is never as exciting as evidence of an expanding economy.

– *Open Horizons*, 218–19

Should the time ever come when we allow our engrossment with comfort and technological progress to erase our longings to the point where we no longer dream of an unspoiled world, then I fear for America.

– *Open Horizons*, 224

There are those who believe we can have our high technology, continue at the same pace, and still preserve our world. I doubt that this will be possible. The only alternative is to reverse our dominant attitude toward the earth and in our use of it recognize that man is part of nature, and that his welfare depends as it always has and always will on living in harmony with it.

– *Open Horizons*, 225

Man's problem today is more than escape from the world; he must understand the reason for his discontent and know that while his roots may have been severed, they can be nourished again by nature if he is aware of its true meanings. He must believe that the spiritual values which once sustained him are still there in those parts of the world he has not ravished, and that they can return again when the wounds of the land are healed.

– *Open Horizons*, 226

If we can move into an open horizon where we can live in our modern world with the ancient dreams that have always stirred us, then our work will have been done.

– *Open Horizons*, 227

We know our basic human needs, that man is part of all that had gone before, his hunger and discontent an inescapable longing for the old simplicities he once knew, that we are in truth children of the earth and cannot change. It is wholeness we are seeking, and being in tune with ancient rhythms and the intangible values of a life we have abandoned.

– *Reflections from the North Country*, 7

There is a certain dignity that comes to those who use their hands in doing something well, a calm assurance at having conceived an object and seeing it through to its completion, which is missing in production lines where workers often do only one essential task and never see the finished product.

– *Reflections from the North Country*, 108

What we have lost in the process of mechanization is the simple fact there can be a joy in work that is found no other way. Labor, no matter what it is, can be its own reward. It does not have to be a work of art, or creative in the sense of involving mind and imagination, but if one looks at it as contributing to the general welfare, the most menial task can be worthwhile and add a certain dignity. No task need consume a mind entirely; one can think and dream even though the body is committed. There is also no reason a man doing dull physical work cannot, during his evenings or whenever he happens to be free, enjoy music, literature, or some artistic pursuit of his own; no reason work as an ethic should be the sum total of existence.

— *Reflections from the North Country,* 109

A basic ecological truth which we still ignore is the interdependence and interaction of all living things, including man. This is the guiding principle underlying human destiny, and we know unless we choose wisely in the few decades ahead, the fragile and intricate web of life could become a web of death.

— *Reflections from the North Country,* 139

Only when we look at the earth as civilized thinking men with enlightened insight will the full measure of human evolution be possible. Man's problem is far more than escape from his predicament; he must know the reasons for his discontent and, in spite of having been torn from his old environment, realize the values which once sustained him are still there in those parts of the world he has not ravished.

— *Reflections from the North Country,* 171

A Breath of Wind

This chapter contains some of Sigurd Olson's best pure nature writing about things that meant much to him: the sun, the moon, and the sky, lakes and rivers, the seasons, loons, cabins, portages, and his favorite outdoor activities. (For the topic of wolves, see the chapter "Saving the Pieces.") But not all of the quotations were chosen for beauty's sake—some of them were included to give a sense of immediacy or to give a fuller indication of his views and how they developed over time. This latter goal is especially important in the section on hunting and fishing, a theme that seems to prove very difficult for many people who otherwise love Olson's writing. He hunted deer until most of his hunting partners died and it no longer was fun; he hunted ducks until he was well into his seventies. He reveled in hunting and did not see it as incompatible with any of his conservation beliefs. He saw hunting, trapping, and fishing as natural human activities that were among the most ancient human connections to the earth and in no way incompatible with love for nature or a sound land ethic.

Winter

A beautiful winter morning, cold and clear. All of the fogginess and mist has gone and the air is as clear as the bluest ice. It must be forty below at least for on either side of the sun the sundogs are riding like two miniature rainbows, the kind of a morning when I would like to be on my skis skimming along the lake trails. The air alone is enough to make one long for action. Breathing itself is an exhilaration. On mornings such as this in spite of the cold I understand why people will persist in living in the north. South there is never the wild joy of living there is up here.

– Journal, January 17, 1930

A perfectly gorgeous morning after the storm, wind in the south, frost crystals hanging on every bush and twig, a hard crust and over all the brilliant northern sunlight of March. What a morning to hit the trail and take great strides over the country. Valleys would disappear beneath my snowshoes, rivers flow under me, hills seem nothing but molehills, the kind of a morning when distance counts for nothing and one's muscles seem tireless, the kind of day when romance lurks around every corner and it seems good just to be alive and moving.

– Journal, March 9, 1935

There is a moment of suspense when the quiet can be felt, when it presses down on everything and to speak seems a sacrilege. Suddenly the air is white with drifting flakes and the tension is gone. Down they come, settling on the leaves, into crevices in bark, on the lichen-covered rocks, disintegrating immediately into more and more wetness. Then almost magically the ground is no longer brown but speckled with white. Now there is an infinitesimal rustling as the flakes drift into the leaves and duff. Swiftly the whiteness spreads, then the earth is sealed and autumn is gone.

– *The Singing Wilderness*, 192

It is true that simplicity and order had come to the wilderness and a quiet that the months since spring had never known. There was joy and beauty in the winter woods, but there was also suffering and death. Only the strong would survive to bear their young in the spring, but this was the way it had always been.

– *The Singing Wilderness,* 196

It was a beautiful night for travel—twenty below, and the only sound the steady swish and creak of my snowshoes on the crust. There was a great satisfaction in knowing that the wolves were in the country, that it was wild enough and still big enough for them to roam and hunt. That night the wilderness of the Quetico–Superior was what the voyageurs had known two hundred years before, as primitive and unchanged as before discovery.

– *The Singing Wilderness,* 240

Spring

To anyone who has spent a winter in the north and known the depths to which the snow can reach, known the weeks when the mercury stays below zero, the first hint of spring is a major event. You must live in the north to understand it. You cannot just come up for it as you might go to Florida for the sunshine and the surf. To appreciate it, you must wait for it a long time, hope and dream about it, and go through considerable enduring.

– *The Singing Wilderness,* 15–16

As I walked back toward home, the grouse was drumming on its log and the frogs were tuning up in the little pond. The killdeer were quiet now and the blackbirds had gone to sleep, but I heard the song of the hermit thrush, the clear violin notes that in a little while would make every valley alive with music. Spring in the north was worth waiting for and dreaming about for half the year.

– *The Singing Wilderness*, 21

The spruces were full of the soft mating-calls of the chickadees, the sound which more than any other proves that the sun is warm on the south sides of trees, that spring is on the way.

– *The Singing Wilderness*, 29

I had not found the secret of the Chippewas, but I had known for a little while the ancient beauties of their solitudes, the warmth of the April sun, a glittering icy highway, and frost crystals as big as butterflies. I had seen the stars very close, had heard the song of the coyotes and listened to the first full breathing of the lake. I had made medicine with the chickadees and the whisky-jacks, had played a game of hide-and-seek with the ravens, had caught a trout and seen its ghostly flash in the blue-black depths of the lake. I had spent some days as leisurely as a bear coming out of its den, soaking up the warmth of spring.

– *The Singing Wilderness*, 30

Ours was a sense of golden leisure that comes only in the spring, after months of grayness and cold.

– *Runes of the North*, 97

Even in my dreams the creeks and rivers of spring haunted me, the sound of running water, oozing rivulets from suddenly warmed banks, dogwood stems flaming in the sun, the birches of the ridges turning purple in their tops. Arbutus were always blooming on southern slopes, pussy willows swelling over the snow, yellow cowslips brightening the edges of swamps. Then the smells, the bittersweet resins of Balm of Gilead, masses of balsam in the first real warmth, the thawing earth itself, a combination of odors so powerful it was as though the air were surcharged with them. All this colored my days, for this was the awakening and the beginning of life after the long sleep of winter. At times it seemed I too must burst with the swelling buds, grow as they grew, reach for the sun, run over the hills along the streams and through the woods giving vent to the joy and excitement within me.

– *Open Horizons*, 8–9

Summer

Summer begins in June. It comes after the wild excitement of spring, the migration of birds, their mating and choosing of places to live and defend. It is a time of fullness and completion, the goal of all that has gone before. . . . All living creatures gorge themselves and their young on the food that is at this season so rich and abundant. It is a time for building strength and storing energy for whatever may come. It is also a time of joy.

– *Wilderness Days*, 61

In the warmth of rains and sunny days, the forest floor literally teems with life. Seeds swell and burst and grow, colored fungi and lichens all but spring from the ground. Flowers are bolder in their hues than those of spring. They bloom in crannies on cliffs, on bare rock faces, in swamps and forest shades. . . . There is a sense of almost tropical lushness after the stark severities of winter.

– *Wilderness Days*, 61

Because there is so much of everything, there is a relaxation in effort and even time for playing in the sun. In the mornings the mists roll out of the bays, pink when the days are bright, ghostly white when they are dark. In the evenings the loons call, while hermit thrushes and whitethroats warble in the aspen.

– *Wilderness Days*, 61

This is the essence of summer—a time of plenty and a soft green beauty in which hardships, survival, and eternal striving belong to a different and almost forgotten time.

– *Wilderness Days*, 61

Autumn

The leaves are gone from the hillsides and the glory of the red maple and of the yellow aspen and birch is strewn upon the ground. Only in the protected swamps is there any color, the smoky gold of the tamaracks. A week ago those trees were yellow, but now they are dusty and tarnished. These are days of quietly falling needles when after each breath of wind the air is smoky with their drift.

– *The Singing Wilderness*, 171–72

This fall I was on the Island River. It was late October and the tamaracks were as golden as they would ever be. Before me was a stand of wild rice, yellow against the water, and because it was a bluebird day there was not a wing in the sky. I stood there just looking at the horizon. Suddenly the sun went under a cloud and it began to snow, softly at first, and then as the wind rose the serrated ranks of tamaracks across the bay almost disappeared in swirling flakes. A flock of northern bluebills tore out of the sky with that canvas-ripping sound that only bluebills make when they have been riding the tail of the wind and decide to come in. In a split second, an instant in which I was too startled even to move, there were a hundred wings where before there had been nothing but space. Then they were gone and in the same instant the sun came out.

– *The Singing Wilderness*, 174

When the hunting moon of October first appears, it is big and orange and full of strange excitement. Then it is at its best; later it pales, but those first few moments are moments of glory.

– *Runes of the North*, 41

In the fall when the rice harvest is on, I think of canoes going through golden fields of it against the blue of the water, the flash of ducks above and the whisper of their wings, the redolent haze from parching fires over some encampment.

– *Runes of the North*, 119

Sun, Moon, and Sky

When the moon shines as it did last night, I am filled with unrest and the urge to range valleys and climb mountains. I want vistas of moonlit country from high places, must see the silver of roaring rapids and sparkling lakes. At such times I must escape houses

and towns and all that is confining, be a part of the
moon-drenched landscape and its continental sweep.

– *The Singing Wilderness*, 84–85

Under the full moon life is all adventure.

– *The Singing Wilderness*, 85

I thought as I lay there in my bag that, if nothing else,
moonlight made animals and men forget for a little
while the seriousness of living; that there were moments
when life could be good and play the natural outlet for
energy. I knew that if a man could abandon himself as
my deer mouse had done and slide down the face of the
earth in the moonlight once a month—or once a year,
perhaps—it would be good for his soul.

– *The Singing Wilderness*, 89

The lights of the aurora moved and shifted over the
horizon. Sometimes there were shafts of yellow tinged
with green, then masses of evanescence which moved
from east to west and back again. Great streamers of
bluish white zigzagged like a tremendous trembling
curtain from one end of the sky to the other. Streaks of
yellow and orange and red shimmered along the
flowing borders. Never for a moment were they still,
fading until they were almost completely gone, only to
dance forth again in renewed splendor with infinite
combinations and startling patterns of design.

– *The Singing Wilderness*, 183–84

The last rays of the sunset tinted the great boles of the
trees and made them glow with fire.

– *Listening Point*, 13

The thunderhead had climbed high and was pink and white and silvered along its edges. As it moved toward the east, it changed to rose and mauve and then to blood red and purple. The west was now in full color and the water as well, and the spruces etched themselves against the horizon.

– *Listening Point*, 13

We reached the lookout point at last, a bare glaciated knob at the highest and most exposed pinnacle of the ridge. Some hardy maples still held a few brilliant leaves, but a scrub oak in a protected crevice flaunted its mahogany in triumph over the gales. To the south the lake was tinted with the sunset, and beyond were the twinkling lights of town. As dusk descended, the water turned to wine, then to black, and the molten gold below faded into the darkness of the valley.

– *Runes of the North*, 42

A slender scimitar of orange sliced through the mist, first only its thin upper edge, then the whole of its rounded rim. The full moon was trembling and pulsating as it pushed and struggled upward and away from the haze which enveloped it. Now it was half, then three quarters. The mists were subsiding, slipping away from their tenuous hold on the lower rim. At last the moon was free, an oval, glowing ball of orange; the hunting moon of October.

– *Runes of the North*, 43

It was the last day of deer season and one of those breathless dawns that seem to come only in November. I stood outside my cabin and looked at the stars blazing against their background of blue-black sky. In the east was a hint of rose, not enough to brighten the horizon or dim the stars, merely an assurance that daybreak was near. The birds were stirring and the sounds of their cheeping filtered out of the pines. Along the shore of the lake new ice was forming on the rocks.

– *Runes of the North*, 73

During the day, trunks have a glint of reddish brown which toward dusk may heighten and turn to deeper red or copper, but when the Ross light strikes, those boles are changed to gleaming gold, and if there are birch or aspen near by, some of their shimmering whiteness may be washed with it until the trees shine with glowing pink. I have seen a curving shore of birch close to a stand of red pine look as though someone had dipped a soft brush in their color and stroked the fringe of an entire bay.

– *Runes of the North*, 122–23

All who have known the mountains have waited for the alpenglow, when snow-clad peaks turn red for just a moment, and glaciers and streamers of ice hang like colored ribbons from the heights. Long after the valleys are dark, those peaks continue to glow, and as the light recedes, they fade to purple and then to black with only the highest pinnacle flaming to the end.

– *Runes of the North*, 123

Every bit of water had turned to gold and, as the valley darkened, it looked as if molten metal had been spilled and dribbled over the black velvet of the land.

– *Runes of the North*, 123

It had been a wild, blustery day with snow swirling constantly. Toward evening the sun broke through the

gray clouds and, when it washed the rice beds, the fury
was forgotten—the wet and frozen hands, the shivering
in the teeth of the wind—and for a moment there was a
sense of warmth and quiet in which I was no longer
conscious of the storm. Silhouetted against the lowering
sky that evening were flights of ducks and in the shaft
of light they became drifting skeins, silver as they
turned, gold as they flew into the west.

– *Runes of the North,* 125

Lakes and Rivers

As I approach the Namekagon, peace comes to me and
I dare not speak save in a whisper. I tread softly,
stopping ever so often to listen. Now I can hear it, the
soft liquid gurgle of clear water washing over rounded
stones. A breath of wind in the aspen and it is gone.
There it comes again, a steady undertone of softness
and sadness. The flash of rapids through the foliage
and then I am at the bank. No, it has not changed as
I had feared. It is as I left it years ago. There before me
is a deep pool swirling smoothly in its depths against
the opposite bank. Here on quiet summer evenings
when the June bugs were out rose great speckled
trout.

. . . One of the reasons I love the Namekagon, it is
so alive. It has its moods, somber in the big quiet pools,
furtive beneath the overhanging banks, mysterious,
dark and gruesome in the deeps, laughing and shouting
in the rapids. How like our own selves they are as they
break away from depth and introspection, from
brooding and disaster, how they break away at last
into lightness and sun, gallop and play with no end but
escape and joyous movement.

. . . Here was peace and quiet, here it did not matter whether the question was answered or not. This was the place to decide, not back there in the heat and turmoil. The quiet almost hurt and the rapids seemed to whisper "We are the same and you are the same, we are the same and you are the same" and as I looked long and long at this river of mine I knew it was so. . . . It had taken twenty years, twenty years of the best of my life to find the answer and now back at the little river it had come to me. No, I knew the only things [that] mattered [were] the feel of sunlight and wind, the smell of fresh earth and kinship with the trees. I had come home at last.

– Journal entry, "The River," ca 1939–1940

A mountain, a desert, or a great forest might serve his need of strength, but water reflects his inner needs. Its all-enveloping quality, its complete diffusion into the surrounding environment, the fact it is never twice quite the same and each approach to it is a new adventure, give it a meaning all its own. Here a man can find himself and all his varied and changing moods.

– Listening Point, 36

I walked to the end of the point and sat down. Long swells washed the rocks, and the chucklings that came from them soon were echoed within myself. As I looked and listened, all the confused hurrying of the day was slowed down and seemed to merge with the quiet movement of the water.

– Listening Point, 37

These witching hours blend one into the other as calm may blend into storm, for water reflects not only clouds

and trees and cliffs, but all the infinite variations of
mind and spirit we bring to it.

– Listening Point, 43

Little rivers, beautiful, wild, and clear, meander through
my dreams.

– *Of Time and Place*, 54

Loons

The loons of Lac la Croix are part of the vast solitudes,
the hundreds of rocky islands, the long reaches of the
lake toward the Maligne, the Snake, and the Namakon.
My memory is full of their calling: in the morning when
the white horses of the mists are galloping out of the bays,
at midday when their long, lazy bugling is part of the
calm, and at dusk when their music joins with that of
the hermit thrushes and the wilderness is going to sleep.

– *The Singing Wilderness*, 38–39

The canoe was drifting off the islands, and the time had
come for the calling, that moment of magic in the north
when all is quiet and the water still iridescent with the
fading glow of sunset. Even the shores seemed hushed
and waiting for that first lone call, and when it came, a
single long-drawn mournful note, the quiet was deeper
than before.

– *Listening Point*, 61

Above came a swift whisper of wings, and as the loons
saw us they called wildly in alarm, increased the speed
of their flight, and took their laughing with them into
the gathering dusk. Then came the answers we had
been waiting for, and the shores echoed and re-echoed

until they seemed to throb with the music. This was the symbol of the lake country, the sound that more than any other typifies the rocks and waters and forests of the wilderness.

– *Listening Point*, 62

The sound of a whippoorwill means an orange moon coming up in the deep south; the warbling of meadowlarks the wide expanses of open prairies with the morning dew still upon them; the liquid notes of a robin before a rain the middle west and east; the screaming of Arctic terns the marshes of the far north. But when I hear the wild rollicking laughter of a loon, no matter where I happen to be, it means only one place in the world to me—the wilderness lake country and Listening Point.

– *Listening Point*, 69

The loons were calling, I can hear them yet, echoes rolling back from the shores and from unknown lakes across the ridges until the dusk seemed alive with their music. This untamed sound, the distances, the feeling of mystery and adventure filled me with joy and elation. . . . I know now why children are sometimes seized with the necessity of expressing their joy in violent physical activity, why they dance and run and climb and tumble until utter weariness makes them pause.

– *Runes of the North*, 20–21

Cabins

When I entered that cabin I was close to the wild. . . . This was no place for fancy or unnecessary equipment. The cabin meant moccasins, rough wool, and leather—

and simple thoughts. The complicated problems of society, politics, war and peace seemed far removed. The only thoughts that thrived here were of squirrels and birds and snowshoe trails. Here I felt as much a part of the out-of-doors as when sleeping under a ledge.

– *The Singing Wilderness*, 205

I have always felt that cabins belong to the animals of the woods as much as they do to us and that the animals should feel as much at home in them as though there were no doors or walls. By shutting them out, we lose their companionship and the feeling of trust which comes only when the barriers of strangeness and fear are overcome.

– *The Singing Wilderness*, 206

Sometimes at night I would waken and listen to the tips of the spruce branches rubbing against the walls, caressing them softly. That cabin was still part of the living forest, would eventually be part of the moss and duff again. At such times my thoughts seemed to merge with the trees and the sound of their movement in the wind, their creaking and moaning as they rubbed against one another.

– *The Singing Wilderness*, 206

There are many trappers' cabins in the north and there are many mansions called cabins. Many of them are comfortable and beautiful in their way, but when I enter them there is no change for me, merely an extension of civilized living away from the towns. Motor boats, highways, and planes make them as accessible as suburban homes. I find no sense of seclusion or solitude in them, for their conveniences carry with them the associations and responsibilities of urban living.

Sometimes they are so comfortable, so removed from all physical effort, that they nullify the real purpose of going to the woods: doing primitive things in primitive ways and recapturing simplicity.

– *The Singing Wilderness*, 208

Trappers' cabins are as natural as tents or teepees. They are part of the solitudes and as much a part of the wilderness as the trees and rocks themselves. In those cabins the wilderness always sings.

– *The Singing Wilderness*, 208

It must be as natural as a shelter back in the bush, like an overhanging ledge or a lean-to, or a cabin on some trapper's route. We would carry water from the lake, cut our firewood, do all the things we would have done in the wilds, and when we went to sleep at night we wanted the feeling that we were still close to the out-of-doors and that the cabin was not merely an extension of our house in town.

We wanted the partridge to walk around it, to come out in the dusk and sit there in the twilight unafraid. We wanted red squirrels spiraling down the trunks of the pines and vaulting onto the roof as though it were part of the trees themselves. Even the deer mice would be welcome to build their nests in some dark corner under the rafters. The chickadees would be part of it, and the soft warbling notes of the whiskey-jacks, and the calling of the loons on the open lake. The wind and the waves and all the sounds of the night would be there. It must be only one room, just large enough for a couple of bunks, a fireplace and a table, as close to the primitive as we could keep it and in harmony with Listening Point.

– *Listening Point*, 18

I have always felt that views through windows leave much to be desired, that to really enjoy a view it should be undimmed by glass or frame. While a scene might be beautiful from the inside, something important is always lost there, for a vista divorced from the open air and the smells and sounds and feelings around you is only partially enjoyed. If we could see all there was to see from indoors, if we became content to have the beauty around us encompassed by the four walls of the cabin, we would lose what we came to find, and that we must never do.

– *Listening Point*, 20

Hunting and Fishing

Bang—Bang—Bang—came from far up stream, someone shooting ahead of time and I cursed inwardly all law breakers in general although I admitted the temptation.

– "Confessions of a Duck Hunter," *Sports Afield*,
  October 1930

Everyone seemed to be getting shooting but me. It was disquieting to say the least, particularly when reflecting that I had hunted deer for almost twenty years, had guided scores of parties myself, and was generally considered an old hand at the game.

– "Stage Pants Galahads," *Sports Afield*,
  November 1930

The sky was clouding up and the wind beginning to moan through the trees. We watched the signs of the coming storm joyfully. If it would only begin to snow, our happiness would be complete. It didn't seem quite natural to have good shooting and good weather too. Storm and ducks had always been one and the same to us.

– "The Blue-Bills Are Coming!" *Sports Afield,*
    October 1931

The prettiest shot we made was on a bunch of five that decoyed after they had flown over us once. The first time 'round, they were just out of range but the second they couldn't have been in more perfect formation. As our guns cracked two tumbled. The remaining three climbed for elevation. Two more shots and there were four on the water and the fifth scooting away with the jerky, panicky flight the ones that get away always seem to have.

– "The Blue-Bills Are Coming!" *Sports Afield,*
    October 1931

There is a certain duck marsh close by where I have spent many hours during the past ten years. I have stood in my blind in the darkness watching the stars fade and the sun rise. I have stood there during many sunsets. Hours on end I have stood there and studied the opposite shoreline until I can truthfully say there is not a stub nor a bush nor a single irregularity in the skyline that I do not recognize and know. I know also just what parts of that shoreline have exploded ducks. Over one clump of old dead tamaracks the mallards always come, and over another the bluebills. And when they come in, from long experience I know what they will do, and they proceed to do it with as much regularity as though they had rehearsed the act many times. I know just what little openings in the rice they are going to drop into and why. I have hunted in many other places where I have gotten many more ducks, but the fact that I know this lake, the fact that the old campsite has many pleasant associations tied up with it, makes a trip there doubly enjoyable.

– "Familiarity," manuscript draft, December 1, 1933

Back from six days of deer hunting, packing and ranging in the brush and what a wonderful feeling there is in this old body of mine. Once again, I feel hard and fit, energy is flowing through my system and I feel as though I could do anything.

– Journal, November 26, 1934

It is a cold blooded game, but it satisfies something within me. This is living, this makes up for nights of bridge, for days of indoor life, for soft beds and comfort. I am a hunter, a fighting man again. I have death in my hands, I am strong on the trail, swift at the chase, my eyes are good, I can see everything. No, I am not the killer, ruthless and obdurate. I love these things and need them. I need them to counteract the many things I do that are not natural. . . . There is a satisfaction which nothing else can equal to bringing down your game. What fun it will be to go back to camp and answer the queries of the boys and how soul satisfying it will be to lay very modestly on the kitchen table a nice piece of liver. Yes, this is living and I am happy.

– "The Drive," January 10, 1937 (unpublished)

For years that opening day had been more or less of a religious rite with us, and we would no more think of missing it, or in any way marring its effect, in the slightest, than we would consciously part with our pet guns or decoys.

– "Taking Us, Dad?" *Field and Stream*, January 1938

As any duck hunter knows, be he worthy of the name, mallards at least once during the fall spell the difference between success and failure.

– "Mallards Are Different," *Field and Stream,*
November 1938

I cleaned my deer carefully, took out the intestines, the heart and the liver, the great bulging stomach full of brouse, warmed my hands against the steaming paunch. The hunt was over and now I had my meat and then while I strung him up to freeze, I was conscious of a feeling of disappointment that it was over [and] that I had killed for sport, but as I sat and looked at my kill, I was also conscious of the old thrill that is always mine when I have been successful, the ancient thrill of getting my game, proving to myself that I am still one with the hunters of the past, that the blood of ancestral hunters of Europe still runs strongly in my veins.

– "The Drive," ca February 1940 (unpublished, different
version than quoted from earlier)

There is something to be said for sitting in a blind with the flocks careening over the far horizon and then breaking away and heading in like a flight of bombers and you crouching there waiting for the moment when they'll be in range. Yes, there is something to be said for the excitement that is yours when the air is full of wings and the sound of them, and you have a chance to choose in a split second which one of the entire flock you want to bring down. And there is a lot to be said for that breathless all-gone feeling that is yours when the flight is over and you are once more alone in the blind and a couple of nice ducks are lying out there fanning their wings just beyond the decoys.

– "I'm a Jump Shooter," *Sports Afield,* October 1944

That made five and was enough. One of them was a beautiful greenhead. It lay where it had fallen, stone dead, its emerald head unruffled, the bronze breast feathers unsmudged with blood or mud. Even the little curl of its tail was intact. The bird was perfect as they come, and I lifted it out almost reverently and laid it beside the other four.

– "I'm a Jump Shooter," *Sports Afield*, October 1944

The fishing for fishing's sake alone soon becomes mechanical; and no matter how ideal other conditions may be, the fisherman leaves dissatisfied.

– "Reflections of a Guide," *Field and Stream*,
June 1928

Summer trout from those clear waters are good to look at, but a trout in the spring is a sight to behold—gold and silver with red fins, iridescent in the sun, full-bodied, hard and icy cold as the lake itself.

– *The Singing Wilderness*, 29

We set up the reflector oven, made a pot of tea, prepared the trout. Never had fish been readied with such care or fried with such devotion. When they were the exact shade of golden brown, they were garnished with clusters of red wintergreen berries that had survived the snow. Hot biscuits, a pot of tea, and trout from the icy waters of early spring—who can place a price tag on anything so wonderful?

– *The Singing Wilderness*, 42

He waved his rod in salute, and I left him there casting quietly, hiked clear around the pool so I wouldn't spoil his chances with the big one at the far end. The whitethroats were singing again and high up in the sky the nighthawks were beginning to zoom. There was no wind—a perfect night for a May-fly hatch on the big pool.

– *The Singing Wilderness*, 53

I have always believed that fishing for brook trout is a spiritual thing and that those who engage in it sooner or later are touched with its magic.

– *The Singing Wilderness*, 66

Then, under the light of the kitchen lamp, at a table spread with a new checked cloth, we sit down to a feast of trout and milk and fresh bread, an eighty-year-old lady and a boy of twelve, and talk of robins and spring and the eternal joy of fishing.

– *The Singing Wilderness*, 72

He opened his creel and showed me the beauty on its bed of fern. A nice trout, to be sure, but I knew what his real catch had been that day: the reflections, the coloring, the sounds and the solitudes of which the trout was only a symbol.

– *The Singing Wilderness*, 93

To certain people, speckled trout are more than fish, and the catching of them an aesthetic experience. . . . To the trout fisherman these creatures of spring fed pools and riffles are the loveliest on earth. So beautiful do they seem, it is almost gross to consider eating them. These purists firmly believe that once a man has seen a speckled trout fresh from the water, thrilled to its crimson spots and the mottling of black and green— especially if the taking has been with a dry fly— something has happened to his soul. He has become an artist, a connoisseur, a dealer in rare values and a searcher for the unattainable forever.

– "Of Worms and Fishermen," *Outdoor America*, April 1959

Trout fishing for me is not the taking of fish, but being at one with the stream and all the sights and sounds.

– *Reflections from the North Country*, 34

Skiing

My way of making a trail is a slow one but it is the true trail maker's habit. The first time through it is a case of picking out the easiest ground to travel through. The next it is a case of breaking off the branches that might cut across your frozen face. Each time the trail becomes more and more easy to follow until at last when the track is worn well and all the whipping boughs are broken off you have a highway of your own, one that has never been traveled before, and one that you can close or abandon as you desire. It is the king's highway and you are the king. All the life on either side belongs to you. The scenes are yours because you have made them. Each view is of your own making and enjoyed by you alone. The pictures are not the lifeless ones of art, but can be remodeled or changed as the spirit dictates. Here you are the arbiter of destiny, the lord of all you survey. How few men have a road all of their own that they alone travel and enjoy and how few can afford, once they have so expensive a treasure, to abandon it as I can. I am a millionaire of the spirit.

– Journal, January 22, 1930

Last night the snow was hard and glassy on the south slopes and when coming down a hill the skis would slide as though on glass, but it was beautiful with the reflection and coming down the north slopes where the snow was still powdery, no effort at all, a push on the sticks and you had the sensation of flying.

A flash of white wings behind a bank of snow as though the crest of it had suddenly taken to the air and was winging toward the tree tops—a snowy owl that had drifted down out of the north, the first for many years, flapped its way slowly to the top of a spruce, sat there [like] a ball of white until I was past.

– Journal, March 15, 1941

Each day the trail is different, for the winds have their way with it and sculpture the drifts and tracks of the skis, and when the snow is dry and powdery as the sand of a dune, it is never the same from one moment to the next. Before us the trail is almost obliterated and only in the most protected places is there any sign of travel.

– *The Singing Wilderness*, 226

We leave the high, bare slopes with their shifting snows and glide down into the close intimacy of birch and spruce, the trail winding in and out of thickets, down little slopes and up again, dodging under branches and around rocks and trees with the same feeling that portages give, or game trails, or any primitive paths through unbroken country. Cross-country skiing holds much of surprise and change, but best of all is the feeling of closeness to the woods themselves, to the sounds of birds and trees and the wind.

– *The Singing Wilderness*, 226

Below us are a spruce swamp and a long, winding hill. We push on our sticks and in an instant pick up speed.

The snow has a silky feel to it now, and we weave and
sway around the turns and know the floating lightness
of dancers in ballet. Down through birch and aspen
close enough to touch, around a pine in a swirl of snow,
and suddenly we are in the quiet and deep green of the
spruces.

    – *The Singing Wilderness*, 227

It is much darker as we hurry through the spruces,
and as we climb the hill down which we sped so swiftly
a short time ago long shadows reach across the trail.
At the top we stop to rest, turning to admire the
herringbone pattern of our tracks and the lights playing
across them. The west is in full glow and there are
streamers of apple green and long splashes of orange
and rose. A clump of birch is laced with molten silver.
The mass of the swamp is changing now from dark
green to black and the sky to blood red. Some of the
color is washing onto the lake, the glistening pink
reaches turning to mauve as the edges draw their
purple from the bog.

    – *The Singing Wilderness*, 228

An owl is hooting in the darkening timber, and over the
trees hangs a thin sliver of a moon. It is time to go, and
we drift easily down the old river bed. On the last long
slope we gather speed and know the thrill all skiers
have at night of seeming airborne, of floating down into
the darkness of a bowl. For a fleeting instant we are part
of that glacial river churning through its tunnel of ice,
part of the milky-white water speeding toward the
boulder-strewn outwash below.

    – *The Singing Wilderness*, 229

I remember crisp winter days when I longed to be on my skis. I would get up before daylight and take off for the trails, making it back just in time.

– "The Long Long Dances" (draft of *Open Horizons* chapter),
April 4, 1966

Camping

There is nothing so soul-satisfying and conducive to perfect contentment as a full stomach and a good place to rest, after a day in the brush.

– "Fishin' Jewelry," *Field and Stream,* November 1927

When a man is trying to live another life entirely, he naturally wants to appear as romantic as his conscience will let him. It may be an old checkered shirt or battered hat. Whatever it is, it is usually something in which he thinks he looks or feels particularly well. If it has once become part and parcel of his outdoors life, he will wear it till it falls apart, rather than get a more serviceable garment.

– "Reflections of a Guide," *Field and Stream,*
June 1928

Living happily in the out-of-doors means getting down to the bare essentials. The man who goes in with all of the claptrap necessary to give him a semi-civilized existence in the wilderness is defeating at once the very purpose for which he went in.

– "Search for the Wild," *Sports Afield,*
May–June 1932

There is a bond, stronger than almost anything else, between the men who have sat across campfires in the wilds. No matter what else they may be, the comradeship there is stronger than death.

– Journal, January 28, 1936

So often when we go into the open, we carry our problems with us, not realizing that by so doing we sometimes neutralize the benefits we might derive. If we only allowed the subtle influences of nature to have their way with us unimpeded by anything personal, how much greater would be our benefit. For the outdoors has a way of healing and solving problems and works best where no conscious attempt is made, where no interpretation of any of its moods is even thought of at the time. Somehow and sooner or later, we begin to discover that unconsciously during the time we were out, problems were being solved for us.

– "Spring Morning," *Minneapolis Star-Journal,*
April 20, 1941

One night in a storm I was forced to land on a rocky shore in the full beat of the waves. It was a desperate thing to do, but there was no choice, and when I threw the canoe onto a tangle of matted brush to save it from being pounded to pieces I was assailed by a spicy sweetness that I have never forgotten: the scent of bruised sweet gale. It was so sharp and so totally unexpected that, in spite of the storm and the black and threatening shore where I was forced to camp, it is the outstanding memory of that experience.

– *The Singing Wilderness,* 57

Something happens to a man when he sits before a fire. Strange stirrings take place within him, and a light comes into his eyes which was not there before. An open flame suddenly changes his environment to one of adventure and romance. Even an indoor fireplace has this effect, though its owner is protected by four walls and the assurance that, should the fire go out, his thermostat will keep him warm. No matter where an open fire happens to be, in a city apartment, a primitive cabin, or deep in the wilderness, it weaves its spell.

— *The Singing Wilderness*, 106–7

In years of roaming the wilds, my campfires seem like glowing beads in a long chain of experience. Some of the beads glow more than the others, and when I blow on them ever so softly, they burst into flame. When that happens, I recapture the scenes themselves, pick them out of the almost forgotten limbo of the past and make them live.

— *The Singing Wilderness*, 109

I touched a match to a shred of birchbark, and the little fire that was laid there waiting for this night leaped into the dark. I fed the flames, and they burned as only cedar can, bright and yellow, spitting sparks high above them.

— *Listening Point*, 14

That night it seemed good to crawl into our sleeping bags, to lie there again and listen.

— *The Lonely Land*, 34

After supper the wind grew stronger, but only occasional gusts ruffled the tents. Snug in our bags, we lay listening to the gale overhead, safe and secure in a quiet pocket of the protecting granite ridge behind us. It was good to listen without having to face the force of the blow, good to lie there with rapids behind us and clear going ahead.

— *The Lonely Land*, 70

No one can really appreciate ease without work, or
the luxury of warmth and dryness unless they have
suffered cold and wet under the spur of constant travel.

– *The Lonely Land*, 186

The tents made our camp seem like a little village.
Instead of being hidden by brush and trees, for once
they were out in the open. We walked around from tent
to tent, visiting as though we were on a village square,
the fireplace in the center being common ground.

– *The Lonely Land*, 243

I always look over the gear and the crew before takeoff,
survey the clean outfits, the bulging packs, the untanned
faces, realizing that in a short time all will be changed:
clothes torn, sweat-stained, and spattered with mud
and grease, faces fly-bitten and scratched, canoes,
packs, tents patched and worn and everyone just a bit
wiser than when he went in.

– *Runes of the North*, 134

That day, with an arctic wind sweeping inland from the
ice flows of the straits above, it was so bitterly cold we
could paddle only a few hours at a time without being
forced to land and build a fire. By nightfall, wet and
tired from many rapids and portages, we dragged
our gear into the shelter of a dense grove of spruces
and pitched our camp in an opening beneath them.
Only when the fire blazed high did we discover the
enchantment of the place we had found, a high-ceilinged
room with a golden floor and golden rafters, the walls
huge black boles of trees. Not a gust or breath of wind
disturbed us as we lay basking in the warmth. The
spruces moved and groaned, but we were safe from the
storm, safe and snug as animals in a cave. The day's

adventures, the roaring rapids, loss of equipment, the struggle against the wind and sleet were far away. We ate our food, got into the sleeping bags, and watched the firelight on the canopy above us.

– *Open Horizons,* 31–32

It is one of the secrets of happy travel to see the humor that comes to the surface when it is needed, and is often the saving grace in what could otherwise have been a miserable experience. There is nothing worse than to travel with someone who cannot see the ludicrous in any happening.

– *Reflections from the North Country,* 19–20

Simplicity in all things is the secret of the wilderness and one of its most valuable lessons. It is what we leave behind that is important. I think the matter of simplicity goes further than just food, equipment, and unnecessary gadgets; it goes into the matter of thoughts and objectives as well. When in the wilds, we must not carry our problems with us or the joy is lost. Never indulge in arguments or bitter recriminations; never criticize, but be of good cheer.

– *Reflections from the North Country,* 92–93

Canoes and Canoeing

The movement of a canoe is like a reed in the wind. Silence is part of it, and the sounds of lapping water, bird songs, and wind in the trees. It is part of the medium through which it floats, the sky, the water, the shores.

– *The Singing Wilderness,* 77

A man is part of his canoe and therefore part of all it
knows. The instant he dips a paddle, he flows as it flows,
the canoe yielding to his slightest touch, responsive to
his every whim and thought. The paddle is an extension
of his arm, as his arm is part of his body.

  – *The Singing Wilderness*, 77–78

Should you be lucky enough to be moving across a
calm surface with mirrored clouds, you may have the
sensation of suspension between heaven and earth,
of paddling not on the water but through the skies
themselves.

  – *The Singing Wilderness*, 78

If the waves are rolling and you are forced to make your
way against them, there is the joy of battle, each comber
an enemy to be thwarted, a problem in approach and
defense. A day in the teeth of a gale—dodging from
island to island, fighting one's way along the lee shore
of some wind-swept point, only to dash out again into
the churning water and the full force of the wind, then
to do it again and again—is assurance that your sleep
will be deep and your dreams profound.

  – *The Singing Wilderness*, 79

Almost as great a challenge is running with the waves
down some lake where the wind has a long unbroken
sweep. Riding the rollers takes more than skill with a
paddle; it takes an almost intuitive sense of the weight
and size of them and a knowledge of how they will
break behind you. A bad move may mean that a comber
will wash the gunwales. A man must know not only his
canoe and what it will do, but the meaning of the waves
building up behind him. This is attack from the rear
without a chance of looking back, a guessing at a power

and lifting force that he cannot see. But what a fierce joy to be riding with a thousand white-maned horses racing with the wind down some wild waterway toward the blue horizons!

– *The Singing Wilderness*, 79–80

Is there any suspense that quite compares with that moment of commitment when the canoe heads toward the lip of a long, roaring rapids and then is taken by its unseen power? At first there is no sense of speed, but suddenly you are part of it, involved in spume and spouting rocks. Then when there is no longer any choice and a man knows that his fate is out of hand, his is a sense of fierce abandonment when all the voyageurs of the past join the rapids in their shouting.

– *The Singing Wilderness*, 80

Only fools run rapids, say the Indians, but I know this: as long as there are young men with the light of adventure in their eyes and a touch of wildness in their souls, rapids will be run. . . . I know it is wrong, but I am for the spirit that makes young men do the things they do. I am for the glory that they know.

– *The Singing Wilderness*, 80–81

There is magic in the feel of a paddle and the movement of a canoe, a magic compounded of distance, adventure, solitude, and peace. The way of a canoe is the way of the wilderness and of a freedom almost forgotten. It is an antidote to insecurity, the open door to waterways of ages past and a way of life with profound and abiding satisfactions. When a man is part of his canoe, he is part of all that canoes have ever known.

– *The Singing Wilderness*, 82–83

We would build no boathouse either, for all we would own would be a canoe. We wanted the silences and had no use for larger craft. We could reach the islands in a few minutes of paddling and slip along the shores with nothing to detract from the quiet that was always there.

– Listening Point, 24

It was good to sit there in front of the fire whittling the new paddle. It was elemental work, like shaping a spear or a bow, and when I smoothed the blade and handle I felt nothing could be more vital or important. The very act of shaping it set up a deep-seated chain of subconscious reactions that were satisfying, basic, and primitive.

– Listening Point, 200

It was still a little heavy where the blade fanned out, so I scraped one side and then the other, not enough to weaken it, just what was necessary to bring out the natural resiliency of the wood. A paddle must be elastic, have none of the deadness of too much fiber, must bend when it feels the water. Like a bow, it must be alive, but not so much alive it might break under the strain. There is a fine point beyond which you cannot go, and only one who has used a paddle long can tell when it is reached.

– Listening Point, 201

Paddles mean many things to those who know the hinterlands of the north. They are symbolic of a way of life and of the deep feeling of all voyageurs for the lake and river country they have known.

– Listening Point, 203

It felt good to be cruising again, good to feel the canoes responding to each stroke, to hear the ripple from the bow and the steady swish of our paddles. Our shirts came off and the sun beat on our backs.

– *The Lonely Land*, 24–25

I was up before the east began to glow and in the half light of dawn stood down at the beach watching the whitecaps racing past the point and rolling on toward the north. There was a tail wind, and the day would be good.

– *The Lonely Land*, 36

Running rapids in familiar country is one thing, running them in a strange land where rock formations as well as the speed and depth of the water are different, is another.

– *The Lonely Land*, 57

Within half an hour the bay narrowed and now there was a perceptible movement of the water. The sound we had heard gradually became an all-engulfing roar. It submerged the rising wind, the swish of paddles and the chuckles from the bow. As we moved into its center the old tight feeling within me grew, a feeling I have never overcome and possibly never will. Others may say they approach fast water with calm and assurance, but with me it is always the same. There was no escaping now, no turning back.

– *The Lonely Land*, 59

It was so calm that the canoes seemed to be floating above the water, their reflections as real as the crafts themselves. The shores and islands were double and the flat spit of rock ahead lay like a great spear in the water. A few gulls careened overhead, and loon calls echoed against the hills. A great golden silence lay over the lake. We unconsciously watched our paddles so they would not strike the gunwales and break the spell.

– *The Lonely Land*, 212

Beyond Birch and before Lake Maligne the wind veered completely around and the sun was gone, the sky full of racing black clouds with flashes of lightning between them. Maligne was well named for us—rapids shouting ahead, lightning and thunder, and wild gusts of wind from every point of the compass. Then it was deadly calm, and we sat there somewhat cowed, debating whether to go on or to look for shelter while there was time. All of us had had enough experience to see that evil was brewing; such sudden calm and uncertain gales meant violence. We looked over the shores but they were nothing but swamp—not a high bank or a sign of a rocky shelf, one of those soggy places we always avoided. There was nothing we could do but push on in the hope of finding higher ground before the storm broke. It was a bad decision, for within minutes the sky grew almost black and rain began to fall. Hastily we got out the ponchos, covered the packs, then pushed into the willows as far as we could and sat there waiting for the storm to break. The sky became darker and darker and flashes of lightning burned their way across it. Rolling peals of thunder added the final touch. Ducks flew madly up and down the river; an osprey flew with them, too concerned to think of them as prey. This would have been a beautiful thing to watch from the safety of a snug cabin, but from a canoe in the flooded willows with the river heaving beneath us, it was far from comfortable. A bolt of lightning hit a stub so close to shore we could smell it and feel the tension in the air. The storm was more violent than anything we had ever experienced in the Rainy Lake country or anywhere else.

– *The Lonely Land*, 218–19

It was a joy to see the canoes moving like dancers through intricate steps, weaving, backing, hesitating for a moment, only to dart forward again, thrusting and feinting at times like fencers testing their opponents.

– *The Lonely Land*, 241

I feel about aluminums as you do, somehow they don't quite fit in even though they are rugged and can take punishment.

– Letter to Bill Sheldon, September 14, 1961

Portages

No two portages are alike; each has a character and definite personality of its own, developed partly through our own individual associations with it and partly through its past history.

– "The Romance of Portages," *Minnesota Conservationist*, April 1936

On the portages, we feel at home with the country and it is here we really know the wild.

– "The Romance of Portages," *Minnesota Conservationist*, April 1936

And hardened though a woodsman may be and loath to admit it, still deep down within his rough exterior is an appreciation of setting and atmosphere that is second to none, and old portages to him are sacred.

– "The Romance of Portages," *Minnesota Conservationist,*
April 1936

Deprive a country or a portage of its atmosphere by too much artificialization and you have taken from it its personality, for one is empty without the other.

– "The Romance of Portages," *Minnesota Conservationist,*
April 1936

One might as well try and improve an old masterpiece mellowed by age as try and improve a portage that has been used for centuries.

– "The Romance of Portages," *Minnesota Conservationist,*
April 1936

What is needed is a new conception and appreciation of the meaning of portages. If we look at them in the light of old associations and as monuments to the days of the past, we see more than a carry between two lakes, a place of work or rest. We see them as the ancient wilderness roads of a race, relics of an adventurous past, rarities which in our time are becoming exceedingly precious.

– "The Romance of Portages," *Minnesota Conservationist,*
April 1936

These portage trails of ours are part and parcel of a priceless spiritual heritage, the old wilderness.

– "The Romance of Portages," *Minnesota Conservationist,*
April 1936

THE POWER OF WONDER

Sigurd Olson believed humans have a biological attachment to nature formed during the course of our evolution. Urbanization has cut us off from our biological roots, he said, and the psychological and spiritual restlessness so evident in modern society is due in part to the instinctual longing we still feel for the intimate connection to the earth that our species once enjoyed. He called this longing "racial memory," and it formed the biological underpinning to his later ideas about wilderness as a key component of mankind's continuing spiritual evolution.

This chapter begins by looking at the concept of racial memory as Olson described it over the years and then at various aspects of his antidote to the longing caused by racial memory—spending time in nature. Silence and solitude provide the environmental conditions we need to get the full benefits from reconnecting with the natural world; awareness also is necessary, and a broad base of knowledge can greatly enhance the experience. The benefits include a new sense of time, mystery, wonder, and other immeasurable joys—Olson's "intangibles." The ideal experiences are those that give us a sense of total connectedness or oneness with creation, providing us with momentary epiphanies, or "flashes of insight." These can give us a quiet, lasting joy and a more balanced perspective on life.

Racial Memory

We all have a pronounced streak of the primitive set deep within us, an instinctive longing that compels us to leave the confines of civilization and bury ourselves periodically in the most inaccessible spots we can penetrate.

– "Reflections of a Guide," *Field and Stream*, June 1928

To most men the wild and contact with it are a necessary part of existence. To some it means more than to others, all depending upon the potency of their primitive inheritance. . . . The penalty for disregard is too severe and self-denial when the call is strong results inevitably in frayed nerves, loss of enthusiasm and appetite for present modes of existence. The urge to escape the rush and unnaturalness of urban life and make intimate and forceful contact with the earth once more is a more powerful incentive than most men care to admit even to themselves.

– "Search for the Wild," *Sports Afield*, May–June 1932

The love of the simple life and the primitive . . . is still deeply rooted and it will be hundreds or thousands of years before we lose very much of it.

– "Search for the Wild," *Sports Afield*, May–June 1932

Racial memory is a tenacious thing, and for some it is always easy to slip back into the deep grooves of the past. What we feel most deeply are those things which as a race we have been doing the longest, and the hunger men feel for the wilds and a roving life is natural evidence of the need of repeating a plan of existence that for untold centuries was common practice. It is still in our blood and many more centuries must pass before we lose much of its hold.

– "Why Wilderness?" *American Forests,* September 1938

Uncounted centuries of the primitive have left their mark upon us, and civilization has not changed emotional needs that were ours before the dawn of history.

– *The Singing Wilderness,* 7

The smell of resins is part of our background, part of the woods existence of our ancestors in the pine forests of other continents. Our response to them is part of our racial awareness; our subconscious is so impregnated with them, the memories they invoke are so involved with our ancient way of life that no amount of city-dwelling removed from the out-of-doors will ever completely erase them.

– *The Singing Wilderness,* 56

The fact is that modern man in spite of his seeming urbanity and sophistication is still a primitive roaming the forests of his range, killing his meat, scratching the earth with a stick, gathering nuts and fruits, and harvesting grain between the stumps of burned-out trees, and the old fears as well as the basic satisfactions are still very much a part of him.

– "The Wilderness Concept," speech presented at a meeting of the International Union for the Protection of Nature, Edinburgh, Scotland, June 1956

Though to modern man the music seems to have changed, he still listens to the ancient rhythms. His are the old fears as well as the basic satisfactions, and because of them there is a powerful nostalgia for the wild. While the great silences are now shattered by the roar of jets, the cities he has built vibrating with noise, natural smells replaced by those of combustion and industry, senses bombarded with new and violent impressions, he is still attuned to woods and fields and waters. He has come a long way from the primitive, but not far enough to forget. Were it not for a nature steeped in a racial experience that knew nothing of these things, his adjustment might be swift, but adaptations take eons of time, and mental and physiological processes that have been maturing slowly for a million years cannot be ignored at will. Man of the Atomic Age and its conflicting ideologies is still part of the past.

– *Listening Point*, 241

We have not forgotten these ways, however, for genetic structures, mutations, and adaptations move very slowly, and within us all there is still evidence of a primitive life which left its indelible mark—far deeper, perhaps, than those of the recent frontiers so fresh in our memories.

– *Reflections from the North Country*, 5

Intuition is the response of the subconscious mind arising from the depths of that vast pool of racial awareness which encompasses all experience, not only of our own species but of the forms from which we have come.

– *Reflections from the North Country*, 21

It is when one reaches down into the dark realms of the past that great ideas surge forth.

– *Reflections from the North Country*, 24–25

Silence and Solitude

We sit in silence drinking in the radiant glory about us.
Words would have been sacrilege.

> – "Describes Cruise thru the Woods," *Nashwauk (Minn.) Herald,*
> ca July 1921

The man who has not traveled alone has missed one of
the greatest sources of joy that can come to the lover of
the wilderness. Alone, his perceptions are quickened.
He has no one to look out for his welfare but himself.
This realization gives him a sense of new adventure.
One gets the sensation of traveling alone in a big
uninhabited world. . . . I get much the same sensation
snowshoeing down a frozen lake at night. Nothing to
guide you but a star or two, the shore too far off to be
seen, all alone with the sky and yourself.

> – Journal, March 15, 1932

This was the real wilderness. Here were space and
solitude.

> – "Let's Go Exploring," *Field and Stream,* June 1937

It was before dawn, that period of hush before the birds
had begun to sing. The lake was breathing softly as in
sleep; rising and falling, it seemed to me to absorb like a
great sponge all the sounds of the earth. It was a time of
quiet—no wind rustling the leaves, no lapping of the
water, no calling of animals or birds.

> – *The Singing Wilderness,* 129

At times on quiet waters one does not speak aloud but
only in whispers, for then all noise is sacrilege.

> – *The Singing Wilderness,* 133

Here was the hush; a sense of enormousness and almost crushing silence lay over the land. This was the old Yukon at last.

— *Runes of the North*, 240

Wilderness can be appreciated only by contrast, and solitude understood only when we have been without it. We cannot separate ourselves from society, comradeship, sharing, and love. Unless we can contribute something from wilderness experience, derive some solace or peace to share with others, then the real purpose is defeated.

— *Reflections from the North Country*, 35

One cannot go back for long periods without some personal loss. I discovered this long ago, and have known perimeter men all over the continent who feel the same. Not all of them atrophy; some are keen and delightful, full of joy and without bitterness. But even these men lose something, a certain warmth and humanity, love for others, and the honing of the mind that comes through contact with people. Though they might love other creatures and the land, there is still something missing.

— *Reflections from the North Country*, 36

The great silences are beyond the ordinary sounds of nature, a hush embedded in the deep pool of racial consciousness.

— *Reflections from the North Country*, 37

The great silences mean more than stillness. They are the ancient overpowering silences this planet knew before the advent of modern man. They included the temporary physical sounds of wind and falling water, the roar and crashing of prehistoric creatures, natural in origin and always present.

– *Reflections from the North Country,* 37

Our senses are synchronized to the great quiet by millions of years, making it possible to hear things that today are forgotten. So responsive can we become, even the slightest movement of grasses, leaves, or insects is part of our awareness, until it seems we are hearing with our skin, our sight, smell, and touch, for these are part of the overall pervading silences of the past.

– *Reflections from the North Country,* 40

Awareness and Knowledge

Early morning in the wilderness is the time for smells. Before senses have become contaminated with common odors, while they are still aware and receptive, is the time to go hunting. Winnow in the morning air before it is adulterated with the winds and the full blaze of sunlight, and, no matter where you happen to be, you will find something worth remembering.

– *The Singing Wilderness,* 54

Children live in a world not only of their own, but peopled with all they imagine. Their lives are rich and colored because of it, just as those of adults are enriched by their knowledge of all that has gone before. But the young have a special faculty of listening and understanding and are conscious of the unseen.

– *Open Horizons,* 17

Such vivid awareness is swiftly lost today, but if it can be held into adulthood it enriches and colors all we do.

How often in the wild country of the north I have been
aware of the spirits of the voyageurs, the shadowy
forms that once roamed the rivers and lakes. Often at
night it seemed I could hear ghostly songs coming
across the water, the rhythmic dip of paddles and the
swish of great canoes as they went by.

– *Open Horizons*, 19

Pipes of Pan, the little people, the spirits of trees, of
animals and birds, of rocks and waters, of sun, wind,
and storm, of night and morning, of a world all but
forgotten in the hard, cold light of the technological
civilization we have built; these were part of my early
childhood, a time before reason and knowledge colored
perception, days that not only were mine, but belonged
to the childhood of the race.

– *Open Horizons*, 19

Joys come from simple and natural things, mists over
meadows, sunlight on leaves, the path of the moon over
water. Even rain and wind and stormy clouds bring joy,
just as knowing animals and flowers and where they
live. Such things are where you find them, and belong
to the aware and alive. They require little scientific
knowledge, but bring in their train an ecological
perspective, and a way of looking at the world.

– *Open Horizons*, 170

If I knew all there is to know about a golden arctic
poppy growing on a rocky ledge in the Far North, I
would know the whole story of evolution and creation.

– *Reflections from the North Country*, 67

Often I think of a professor of mine, a great naturalist
and one of the pioneers of our present concepts of plant

and animal ecology, who usually forgot the names of
plants, insects, and birds we encountered on our various
field trips. One day, puzzled at his lack of knowledge,
I asked why he did not know the names, and I shall
never forget his answer: "I am more interested in
broad ecological concepts. I can hire dozens of smart
taxonomists who are encyclopedias of the names of
living creatures. When I need them, I call, but I cannot
clutter my mind with inessentials. It is enough to
know how living things fit into the great scheme of
interrelationships." Too much attention to scientific
detail can rob one of awareness and deeper meanings.

– *Reflections from the North Country*, 69–70

Balance and Harmony

Under ideal conditions, I have seen tourists entranced
at the beauty of a heavily timbered rock point jutting
out into a wilderness lake. Again, I have seen them
curse roundly at the same point and at the waves
breaking over it. A man's point of view determines
whether or not waves are "white-capped billows
rolling in the sun" or just so much damned water to
be paddled through.

The most beautiful scenery is always seen after a
meal. Then, more than at any other time, is a man at
peace with the world and most receptive to all its
wonders.

– "Reflections of a Guide," *Field and Stream*, June 1928

The same sun shines everywhere and the same moon
and the wind. One place is as wild as the other and as
beautiful if one can only see with eyes that understand.

– Journal, February 20, 1940

All sounds were muted. The air lay like a cushion over the grass and the trees and the slow swell that moved rhythmically into the bay. I stood there and listened and felt as though all the world were in slow motion and that I must not hurry or make a sound that might disturb it.

– *Listening Point*, 192

In a world seething with mistrust, suspicion and clashing ideologies, pussy willows may be vital to the welfare of man and his serenity.

– *Listening Point*, 227

Harmony is the musical flow of environmental awareness and evolutional knowledge through the mind of man.

– *Reflections from the North Country*, 61

In wilderness, harmony is the natural way of life as it has always been, but we must not destroy it by overcrowding or by any exploitative use that might change it. The most important function of the wilderness for modern man is the opportunity of glimpsing for a moment what harmony really means. Having sensed it, he can bring the vision back to our urban complexes, and the wisdom that enables us to understand what we have lost.

– *Reflections from the North Country*, 62

Aware at last of our relentless drive for economic development and an ever-higher standard of living at the expense of dwindling resources, and the swiftly mounting degradation of environment and beauty of the natural scene, we are beginning to realize our future course can no longer be at the expense of quality in our lives. Only when we see ourselves as members of a balanced community can we live successfully.

– *Reflections from the North Country,* 139

Time

To that boulder the trees were as grass. It lay among them huge and gray and permanent, had been there thousands of years before they came, would be there long after they were gone.

– *Listening Point,* 13

A year is such a long time to a boy!

– *Open Horizons,* 25

When one finally arrives at the point where schedules are forgotten, and becomes immersed in ancient rhythms, one begins to live.

– *Reflections from the North Country,* 27

In the wilderness there is never this sense of having to move, never the feeling of boredom if nothing dramatic happens. Time moves slowly, as it should, for it is a part of beauty that cannot be hurried if it is to be understood. Without this easy flowing, life can become empty and hectic.

– *Reflections from the North Country,* 29

We cannot all live in the wilderness, or even close to it, but we can, no matter where we spend our lives, remember the background which shaped this sense of the eternal rhythm, remember that days, no matter how frenzied their pace, can be calm and unhurried. Knowing we can be calm and unhurried we can refuse

to be caught in the so-called rat race and the tension
which kills Godlike leisure. Though conscious of the
roar around us, we can find peace if we remember
we all came from a common mold and primeval
background.

– Reflections from the North Country, 30–31

Mystery and Wonder

While we are born with curiosity and wonder and our
early years full of the adventure they bring, I know such
inherent joys are often lost. I also know that, being deep
within us, their latent glow can be fanned to flame
again by awareness and an open mind.

– Listening Point, 4

The spirit land of the Chippewa, the spirit lands of
all peoples, how important to catch their meaning,
how little we know when we see only rocks and trees
and waters, mountains and meadows and prairies,
how impossible to catch the feeling of any country
without sensing its legendry and the mystery of what
cannot be seen, places that always speak of the
unknown.

– Listening Point, 73

Myriads of stars were my net that night, but I no longer
felt lonely, for I knew that while man might unravel
the puzzled skein of life and solve the riddles of the
universe, what really matters is the wonder which
makes it all possible. Back of everything is always a
net of dreams.

– Runes of the North, 18

The pipes of Pan sound early before the sense of
wonder is dulled, while the world is wet with dew and
still fresh as the morning.

– Open Horizons, 3

My first recollection came one sunny afternoon when
Mother led me through a grove of maples in the fall.
That day the trees must have been in full color, for the
ground was deep in drifting leaves. As we walked
through them we were surrounded with color, and
when the wind blew we were drenched with it. The
swirling masses of red and yellow filled me with
excitement, and when we ran through the grove,
ran and ran until we could run no more and sank
laughing to the ground, color and beauty became part
of my life.

– Open Horizons, 3–4

The power of wonder and the unknown are intangibles
we must cherish if we are to comprehend our problems.
In them was the wellspring of our dawning culture,
and from it the first significant expressions of man's
mind. Without its spur, scientists, artists, and workers
in all disciplines of creative endeavor would lose the
challenge to probe and explore. An infallible source of
inspiration, it is rooted in man's contemplation of his
environment. When we create life, find all the secrets of
the universe, and progress to other planets, wonder will
have been responsible.

If wonder is one of man's great potentials, playing
a major role in the progression of his thinking and
knowledge, and unspoiled nature a means of invoking
it, here is reason enough for preservation.

– Open Horizons, 223

If we can somehow retain places where we can always sense the mystery of the unknown, our lives will be richer.

– *Reflections from the North Country*, 42

If you lose the power of wonder, you grow old, no matter how old you are. If you *have* the power of wonder, you are forever young—the whole world is pristine and new and exciting.

– In *The Wilderness World of Sigurd F. Olson*, Twin Cities Public Television, 1980

Intangible Values

I do not ever hope to accumulate worldly wealth, but I shall accumulate something far more valuable, a store of wonderful memories.

– "Describes Cruise thru the Woods," *Nashwauk (Minn.) Herald*, ca July 1921

When in the wilderness, all else is forgotten. He does not count as wasted any time spent watching the clouds, the trees, or the waters. To him, those hours are precious, for it is then that he is storing up a wealth of memories that will help him tide over the times when the stress of city life bears too heavily upon him, and make him forget the struggle in a vision of clear blue skies and sunlit woods and waters.

– "Reflections of a Guide," *Field and Stream*, June 1928

It felt good to feel the north wind, to face it and glory in it. There was no bite to it, merely a good fierce joy in the sting of it.

– Journal, December 12, 1934

I have stood on top of a windswept hill, waved my hat
at the breeze, shouted to the skies that I was alive, and
I have fought the waves on gigantic lakes and enjoyed
the slap of every one. I love the rain, the snow, thunder,
storms, quiet, every change of the weather. That is all
part of the picture. Outdoors everything has its place,
everything contributes toward the sum total of
enjoyment.

– Journal, March 4, 1935

Intangible values are those which stir the emotions,
that influence our happiness and content, values that
make life worth living. They are all tied up with the
idea of the good life. Sometimes I wonder if we actually
know what the good life means. But this we know—that
whatever it is, the intangible values are so important
that without them life loses its meaning.

– "Those Intangible Things," Izaak Walton League of America
convention, early 1954

It is hard to place a price tag on these things, on the
sounds and smells and memories of the out-of-doors,
on the countless things we have seen and loved. They
are the dividends of the good life.

– "Those Intangible Things," Izaak Walton League of America
convention, early 1954

What is their nature, and how shall we know them
when they come? The truth is, they cannot be defined,
described, or measured, only felt—so simple and
self-evident they are often unknown. Such intangible
values stir the emotions, influence happiness and
content, make life worth living, give richness, color,
and meaning to all we do. One cannot explain why a
painting thrills us, or a symphony, a poem, a friendship,

or love of the land, a corner of wilderness, or the words "Thy rocks and rills, thy woods and templed hills," but we know inherently what they mean.

Such things give dignity and purpose to life; they are part of solitude, tranquility, and silence, the sense of oneness with living things, and the awe with which we look at the world. No one has ever listed them, but each encompasses the others. They speak to us in such immortal lines as "He leadeth me beside the still waters, He restoreth my soul," or "I lift up mine eyes unto the hills, from whence cometh my help," and we intuitively sense their meaning, and share in a response that has its origins in the primal hunger of all men for beauty, peace, and order. This is what the psalmists felt as they looked with joy and wonder at the landscape of the universe.

– *Open Horizons*, 222–23

Connectedness

Most of all would I find what I sought on brilliant starlit nights. I would paddle out swiftly onto the open lake if the moon was shining down its path. It never failed to come to me when going down that brilliant shining highway into space. Most completely of all would I be taken when lying on my back looking at the stars. The gentle motion of the canoe softly swaying, the sense of space and infinity given by the stars, gave me the sensation of being suspended in the ether. My body had no weight, my soul was detached and I careened freely through a delightfulness of infinite distance. . . . Sometimes the night cry of the loon would enhance the illusion. For long periods, I would lie having lost track of time and location. A slap of a wavelet would jerk me back into the present and I would paddle back to the glowing coals of the deserted campfire, there to sit gazing into the coals trying to fathom the depths of the experience I had been through.

– Journal, January 20, 1930

A school of perch darted in and out of the rocks. They were green and gold and black, and I was fascinated by their beauty. Seagulls wheeled and cried above me. Waves crashed against the pier. I was alone in a wild and lovely place, part at last of the wind and the water, part of the dark forest through which I had come, and of all the wild sounds and colors and feelings of the place I had found. That day I entered into a life of indescribable beauty and delight. There I believe I heard the singing wilderness for the first time.

– *The Singing Wilderness*, 8

He was part of the rocks and trees and the music of running water.

– *The Singing Wilderness*, 49

I once climbed a great ridge called Robinson Peak to watch the sunset and to get a view of the lakes and rivers below, the rugged hills and valleys of the Quetico–Superior. When I reached the bald knob of the peak the sun was just above the horizon, a flaming ball ready to drop into the dusk below. Far beneath me on a point of pines reaching into the lake was the white inverted V of my tent. It looked very tiny down there where it was almost night.

As I watched and listened, I became conscious of the slow, steady hum of millions of insects and through it the calling of the whitethroats and the violin notes of the hermit thrushes. But it all seemed very vague from that height and very far away, and gradually they merged one with another, blending in a great enveloping softness of sound no louder, it seemed, than my breathing.

The sun was trembling now on the edge of the ridge. It was alive, almost fluid and pulsating, and as I watched it sink I thought that I could feel the earth turning from it, actually feel its rotation. Over all was the silence of the wilderness, that sense of oneness which comes only when there are no distracting sights or sounds, when we listen with inward ears and see with inward eyes, when we feel and are aware with our entire beings rather than our senses.

– *The Singing Wilderness,* 130–31

I sat there a long time and listened to the sounds of the great marsh, the rustle of reeds and grasses, the lap of water, the far calling of loons, and finally must have dozed. When I woke, the moon was high and a path of glittering silver lay across the lake.

– *The Lonely Land,* 269

I know there are moments of insight when ancient truths do stand out more vividly, and one senses anew his relationship to the earth and to all life.

– *Runes of the North,* 3

It was sunset when we crossed the last portage around the rapids of the Knife River and stood at last on the shores of the lake itself. A golden glow lay over the water and over our minds as well, and as I looked down that dusky waterway for the first time, saw its rocky islands floating in the distance against the haze of high terrain to the east, I was aware of a fusion with the country, an overwhelming sense of completion in which all my hopes and experiences seemed crystallized into one shining vision.

– *Runes of the North,* 20

I swung the axe again and cut into the raw resin of a
root. The grain was fine and golden yellow and, because
my axe was sharp, its surface gleamed. There was the
embodiment of all that was elemental and afforded me,
a man of the space age, a tie with the past. That root
which once anchored a pine against the gales, held me
to the earth.

    – *Runes of the North,* 72

Once during a violent midsummer storm, the sky grew
black as night and flashes of lightning sliced their
jagged way through it, thunder pealed and rolled
ominously, and at times there was an awesome and
frightening stillness. Sheltered between the huge
buttressing roots of a big pine, I lay there waiting for
the wind to strike. It came in an all-engulfing roar
through the high tops, and as the pine swayed, its
roots moved too. The gale increased, the great trees
bent to and fro and the earth trembled beneath them.
There was a tremendous crash as one of the largest
lost hold and fell, the ground shuddering with its
impact. Then another leaned nearby and I watched as
it slowly moved downward, bringing with it a shower
of bark and branches. At that moment I knew fear and
wonder and an inner exaltation I was to know again
and again through life, a sense compounded of being
one with the elements, the trees, and the wild forces
they bow to.

    – *Open Horizons,* 30–31

When I hear the hermit thrushes and whitethroats at
dusk and the loons calling and a great quiet comes, then
deep within me is the answer.

    – Letter to Reverend Robert Gamble, July 4, 1971

Snatches of high insight, glimpses of beauty, stirrings
of passion, excitement, or enthusiasm, communion with
God may come when we are in harmony with the
whole, at any time—in the eyes of a loved one, or the
touch of a hand. . . . The important thing is to be
aware—never a day without some event that springs
of the spirit.

– *Reflections from the North Country,* 132

Once on an early spring trip, when the snow was
disappearing from the hillsides, the deer were migrating
to the thawed places for food, and the snow on the ice
of lakes had hardened into a firm crust, I sat in front of
my log cabin facing a bay in the east. My companions
had gone to fish for trout and would not return for
several hours. I looked down the lake in the direction
they had gone and lost sight of them as they passed
through a narrows. For some reason I did not return to
the cabin at once: the old silence was there, the sense of
aloneness and oneness. A word would have spoiled it,
but in that special moment the wilderness about me
seemed unutterably clear and close, beautiful and
serene. The moment was short-lived but long enough to
know here again was a flash of reality. I had stayed
behind to cut some firewood, clean the cabin, and find
fresh balsam boughs for the bunks. The chores had new
significance now, the boughs were more resinous and
fragrant, the chopping was a labor of love.

– *Reflections from the North Country,* 134

Unplanned contemplation comes softly as falling mist,
or the first snows of autumn.

– *Reflections from the North Country,* 148

WILDERNESS

Sigurd Olson's early wilderness experiences in the canoe country of northern Minnesota and Ontario during the 1920s gave him glimpses of a deeper meaning to life, a meaning he had been desperately searching for after he could no longer hold onto the Baptist faith of his childhood and youth. And during his summers as a guide, he saw how his clients were transformed in the wilderness. They gradually dropped the hard shells of their business personas and began to laugh and sing and experience the same deep peace Sigurd had found. Like him, they became reconnected to the grand, eternal mystery of creation.

He came to believe his life's mission was to help others find what he had discovered in the wilderness and to fight to preserve wild places wherever they still existed. This chapter begins with some of his key statements about the importance and meaning of wilderness. His earliest articles in the 1920s tended to emphasize the physical advantages of a wilderness trip, but it wasn't long before he began focusing on the spiritual values. After the sections on physical and spiritual benefits is one that examines the value that human history and memories of friends and loved ones adds to a wilderness trip. Perhaps because Olson believed that the primary reason for preserving wilderness was for its effects on the human spirit, he, more than other leading wilderness writers and thinkers, wrote and talked about the significance of these connections to our personal and communal past. This section is followed by a selection of quotations addressing his views about the relationship between wilderness and civilization.

Then this chapter switches gears to look at some of his general remarks about the preservation and management of wilderness—the economic arguments used in wilderness battles, principles of wilderness management, and his comments on three specific aspects: logging, planes, and motorboats. The next chapter includes a number of related statements that focus specifically on the Quetico–Superior canoe country.

Need

Beautiful country, unspoiled country today is something sacred. It is so easy to rob a wilderness of its charm, so hard to bring it back.

– From draft of untitled speech, ca 1934

In some men, the need of unbroken country, primitive conditions, and intimate contact with the earth is a deeply rooted cancer gnawing forever at the illusion of contentment with things as they are. . . . I have seen the hunger in their eyes, the torturing hunger for action, distance, and solitude, and a chance to live as they will. I know these men and the craving that is theirs; I know also that in the world today there are only two types of experience which can put their minds at peace, the way of wilderness or the way of war.

– "Why Wilderness?" *American Forests,* September 1938

I believe this need of wilderness is inherent in most of us, even those seemingly farthest removed from it by civilized living. The cities may cover it up, make us forget temporarily; but deep underneath is an inherent urge for naturalness and simplicity and a way of life different from the one we know.

– "We Need Wilderness," *National Parks Magazine,*
January–March 1946

Some can find their wildernesses in tiny hidden corners where, through accident rather than design, man has saved just a breath of the primeval America. I know of a glen in the heart of a great city park system, a tiny roaring canyon where many seeking solitude and beauty can find release. . . . There, if a man wishes, he can regain in a swift moment the feeling of the wild, and steal, for a brief instant, respite from the noise and confusion of a big city. There, if he has perspective, he may recharge his soul.

– "We Need Wilderness," *National Parks Magazine,*
January–March 1946

Should we forsake these last remnants of our background and sever all tangible ties with the past, then we abandon the nebulous dreams and aspirations, the long gropings of mankind for meaning in the universe which formed him. Should we divorce ourselves physically from those influences that through the ages have molded the body, the mind, and the spirit of man, then like plants whose roots have been cut, we shall wither and die.

– "The Wilderness Concept," speech presented at a meeting
of the International Union for the Protection of Nature,
Edinburgh, Scotland, June 1956

And so it must be for all of us who have known the back country. No little sanctuaries along the fringes of civilization ever quite suffice. We must know the wild and all it entails, the bite of a tumpline on the portages, the desperate battling on stormy lakes, the danger and roar of rapids and falls. We must know hunger and thirst and privation and the companionship of men on the outtrails of the world, for all these things are inseparable. When after days or weeks of travel we modern voyageurs find ourselves on a glaciated point a hundred or a thousand miles from any town and stand there gazing down the length of some unnamed lake listening to the wild calling of the loons and watching the islands floating in the sunset, there is a fierce joy in our hearts.

– *Listening Point*, 238

As long as they remain, as long as there are any places left at all where man can still glimpse the unknown, he will be drawn irresistibly as he has been for ages past, and, seeing them, will wonder and dream and think long thoughts.

– *Listening Point*, 239

The criticism that only a small minority of the population ever has such intimate physical contact with the wilderness way of life is relatively unimportant. . . . the very existence of such areas has an enriching effect not only on adjacent terrain, but on all who glimpse them or are even aware that they exist at all.

– "The Wilderness Concept," *Ames Forester*, 1962 annual

The preservation of wilderness is a humanitarian effort based on the knowledge that man has lived in a natural environment for some two million years and that his physiological and psychic needs come from it.

– "What Is Wilderness?" *Living Wilderness*, Spring 1968

Physical Values

The lives of those who live close to nature in the northland are filled with adventures every day, and to the men of the north they are life. This struggle for existence and the fearless battle with the elements is what makes the manhood of the north big and clean and strong. The north asks for strong men, not weaklings, for here manhood is tested down to the core. To those whom she selects she reveals all her riches, and if she does not give them riches in gold she gives them riches far more worthwhile that mean happiness and contentment.

– "Describes Cruise thru the Woods," *Nashwauk (Minn.) Herald,* ca July 1921

On the other hand, the man who is new cannot get his fill of violent gratification. The long hours of bending to the paddle, oftentimes in the teeth of a gale, and the heart-wrenching work on swampy portages and steep rocky trails are more than compensated for by the feeling that for once he is really alive and living as a man should live. To him there is no joy quite so complete, or content quite so blissful, as that which comes at the end of a killing portage, when he can flop down to rest, half dead of exhaustion.

– "Reflections of a Guide," *Field and Stream,* June 1928

At night, after a long day of cruising through lakes, running rapids, and making portages, his bodily wants satisfied, with nothing ahead but rest and peace under the stars, the full realization comes to him, and then he understands why men go into the wilderness.

– "Reflections of a Guide," *Field and Stream,* June 1928

Spiritual Values

Men realize today that wilderness is a cultural asset, a priceless spiritual heritage necessary to their happiness.

— "Wilderness Areas," *Sports Afield*, August 1938

As it approaches the status of rarity for the first time in history, we see it not as something to be feared and subdued, not as an encumbrance to the advance of civilization, but instead as a distinctly cultural asset which contributes to spiritual satisfaction.

— "Why Wilderness?" *American Forests*, September 1938

I can honestly say that I have heard more laughter in a week out there than in any month in town. Men laugh and sing as naturally as breathing once the strain is gone.

— "Why Wilderness?" *American Forests*, September 1938

Wilderness to the people of America is a spiritual necessity, an antidote to the high pressure of modern life, a means of regaining serenity and equilibrium.

— "We Need Wilderness," *National Parks Magazine*,
January–March 1946

I have found that people go to the wilderness for many things, but the most important of these is perspective. They may think they go for the fishing or the scenery or companionship, but in reality it is something far deeper. They go to the wilderness for the good of their souls.

— "We Need Wilderness," *National Parks Magazine*,
January–March 1946

Important though such experience may be to physical welfare, its most valuable asset is without question in the realm of the spiritual. . . . To countless thousands, wilderness has become a spiritual necessity.

– "The Preservation of Wilderness," *Living Wilderness,*
Autumn 1948

Its understanding and acceptance is so vital a part of our spiritual, cultural, and mental health requirements today that it may well spell the difference between the survival of human dignity in a world of order and beauty and one in which all true values will succumb to the noisy confusions of the atomic age.

– "The Wilderness Concept," speech presented at a meeting
of the International Union for the Protection of Nature,
Edinburgh, Scotland, June 1956

While it is doubtful if our primitive ancestors knew much of the appreciation of the intangible qualities of their environments, we moderns do have that capacity and powers of perception that make it possible to appreciate the qualities of the earth that gave rise to those creative efforts that lifted man gradually from the dark abyss of the primitive to a state where he was able to express his deepest emotions of awe, wonderment, and religious belief in stone and color and finally in words and music. The wilderness concept has to do with the preservation of these wellsprings of the spirit for men of the industrial age.

– "The Wilderness Concept," speech presented at a meeting
of the International Union for the Protection of Nature,
Edinburgh, Scotland, June 1956

We need to preserve a few places, a few samples of primeval country so that when the pace gets too fast we can look at it, think about it, contemplate it, and somehow restore equanimity to our souls.

– "The Meaning of Wilderness," address to Utah Academy of Sciences, Provo, Utah, May 1958

The highest use is the effect these lands have on the spiritual well-being of our people.

– "The Conservation Challenge," address to the Izaak Walton League of America, early 1959

Man's great problem today is to make the transition, to bridge the gap between the old world and the new, to understand the reason for his discontent with things as they are, and to recognize the solution. His old world of superstition, evil spirits, and fear is gone. Gone too his dependence on the wilderness and his sense of close relationship, belonging, and animal oneness with the earth and the life around him. He must recognize now that while some of his spiritual roots have been severed, he still has his gods, and that his attitude toward wilderness has entered a new phase in which for the first time in his evolution as a thinking, perceptive creature, he can look at it with understanding and appreciation of its deeper meanings, knowing that within its borders may be the answer to his longing for naturalness. He needs to know that the spiritual values that once sustained him are still there in the timelessness and majestic rhythms of those parts of the world he has not ravished.

With this realization, wilderness assumes new and great significance. It concerns all of humanity and has philosophical implications that give breadth to the mind and nourish the spirit. Because man's subconscious is steeped in the primitive, looking to the wilderness actually means a coming home to him, a moving into ancient grooves of human and prehuman experience. So powerful is the impact of returning that whether a man realizes it or not, reactions are automatically set in motion that bring in their train an uplift of the spirit. It is as though, tormented by some inner and seemingly unsolvable problem, he is suddenly released from frustration and perplexity and sees his way.

– "The Spiritual Need," at the Ninth Wilderness Conference, San Francisco, April 1965

Wilderness offers this sense of cosmic purpose if we can open our hearts and minds to its possibilities. It may come in such moments of revelation as Aquinas, Chardin, and others speak about, burning instants of truth when everything stands clear. It may come as a slow realization after long periods of waiting. Whenever it comes, life is suddenly illumined, beautiful, and transcendent, and we are filled with awe and deep happiness.

– "The Spiritual Need," at the Ninth Wilderness Conference, San Francisco, April 1965

No longer can [wilderness] be saved from the standpoint of physical enjoyment but only as a stepping stone to cosmic understanding. In a world confused and strident, a world where all the old verities are being questioned, this is the final answer.

– "The Long Long Dances," chapter draft of *Open Horizons,* April 15, 1966

In the saving of places of natural beauty and wildness we are waging a battle for man's spirit.

– "What Is Wilderness?" *Living Wilderness,* Spring 1968

Wilderness is more than camping or hiking; it is a symbol of a way of life that can nourish the spirit.

– "What Is Wilderness?" *Living Wilderness,*
Spring 1968

Life in the wilderness, especially when one is alone, is a continual contemplation and communion with God and Spirit regarding eternal values. One does not have to assume any particular stance, invoke incantations, repeat over and over again words such as "Oom," chant, or sing. To me these are merely hypnotic devices used to bring the mind into focus and into the realm of silence by those who do not have the privilege of living in situations where peace is all about them. There is no doubt of the efficacy of such ways of preparation or they would not be followed by hundreds of thousands, but when quiet is all around, with no sounds but natural ones—bird songs, wind, washing of waters against the shores—the stage is always set for meditation and reflection, whatever one may choose to call it.

– *Reflections from the North Country,* 149

We should preserve our silent sanctuaries, for in them we perpetuate the eternal perspectives.

– *Of Time and Place,* 18

Humans in the Wilderness

The important thing was that for a time they had lived the life of the voyageur and had known the true meaning of peace and the joys of solitude.

– "War Comes to the Quetico," *Sports Afield,*
February 1942

All that is left of those colorful days of the past are crumbling forts, old foundations, and the names the voyageurs gave to lakes and rivers and portages. But there is something that will never be lost; the voyageur as a symbol of a way of life—the gay spirit with which he traveled, his singing as he paddled his canoe, and a love of the wilderness that practically depopulated the struggling pioneer settlements along the St. Lawrence during the heyday of the trade.

– *The Lonely Land*, 10–11

Ghosts of those days stalk the portages and phantom brigades move down the waterways, and it is said that singing still can be heard on quiet nights. I wonder when the final impact of the era is weighed on the scales of time if the voyageur himself will not be remembered longer than anything else. He left a heritage of the spirit that will fire the imaginations of men for centuries to come.

– *The Lonely Land*, 11

That night those men were with us and when the haze of our campfire drifted along the beach, it seemed to join with the smoke of long forgotten fires and lay like a wraith over the canoes, tepees, and tents along the shore.

– *The Lonely Land*, 12

We had no idea of emulating the voyageurs or performing their feats. We had traveled enough together in the Quetico–Superior and other areas to know our limitations. . . . We would paddle the same lakes, however, run the same rapids and pack over the same portages. We would know the wind and the storms and see the same sky lines, and because it was our first expedition into the far Northwest we might feel some of the awe and wonderment and even the fear and delight at the enormous expanses and the grandeur of a new land.

– *The Lonely Land,* 14, 15

While the meaning of wilderness never changes to those who understand it, it means even more if you have sunk your roots in deeply. No country can ever be bleak or forbidding if it has once been a part of the love and warmth of those who have shared it with you.

– *Runes of the North,* 167

Wilderness and Civilization

It was the contrast that fascinated Mac as much as anything else. Knowing that both the wilderness and civilization were available to the nth degree, he was completely happy. I have found it is the same with many men; being able to live in the present and also in the past gives them a sense of completeness that they can get in no other way.

– "Let's Go Exploring," *Field and Stream,* June 1937

I must never write of the earth as being beautiful in itself. Without the civilizing influence of man, without the warmth of godliness and spirit, the earth is merely a cold and brutish planet.

– Journal, November 6, 1940

Civilized living, even though a man may try to escape it, is a great blessing inasmuch as it has made it possible for modern man to get much more enjoyment out of the wilds than his forebears for the simple reason that his perceptions and powers of appreciation are more highly developed.

– "Wilderness Manners," *Sports Afield,* May 1945

Only through my own personal contact with civilization had I learned to value the advantages of solitude. . . . only because of its connotations and the contrasts that had been mine could I really appreciate the wilds and their importance to mankind.

– *Listening Point,* 151

Some other day when the wind was right or the quiet as breathless as this afternoon, I would hear the train again and the steady humming of traffic from the highway. I would remember the time I heard the whistle after that long expedition of years ago and the joy it had brought me then. No longer would I be disturbed, for I would listen now with understanding, knowing what it really meant. Without that long lonesome wail and the culture that had produced it, many things would not be mine—recordings of the world's finest music, books holding the philosophy, the dreams and hopes of all mankind, a car that took me swiftly to the point whenever I felt the need. All these things and countless others civilization had given me, and I must never again forget that because of the wonders it had wrought this richness now was mine.

– *Listening Point,* 152–53

Cultural maturity comes slowly and the old conflicts between materialism and the intangible values will flame on many battlefronts for years to come. When the time arrives that we look at wilderness not as savages, not as pioneer exploiters, but through the eyes of enlightened man with understanding and appreciation of its real meaning, then and only then will the full measure of Thoreau's statement be realized, that "in Wildness is the preservation of the world."

– "The Spiritual Aspects of Wilderness," at the Seventh Biennial Wilderness Conference, San Francisco, April 1961

Wilderness and the Economy

If it contributes to spiritual welfare, if it gives them perspective and a sense of oneness with mountains, forests, or waters, or in any way at all enriches their lives, then the area is beyond price.

– "We Need Wilderness," *National Parks Magazine,* January–March 1946

You can't permit developments within a wilderness area and expect the wilderness to retain its drawing power, but you can locate resorts along the edges of the wilderness, increasing its accessibility and, if anything, increasing the drawing power of the resorts.

– Letter to John Ainley, editor, *Ely (Minn.) Miner,* May 20, 1948

Talk of esthetics and intangible values never seems to measure up to the concrete evidence of swollen payrolls in some isolated community benefiting directly by the exploitation of a hitherto forgotten corner of untouched country.

– "The Preservation of Wilderness," *Living Wilderness,* Autumn 1948

We must stop talking about natural resources, recreational areas, and conservation generally in cold-blooded economic terms, seeing them only as graphs and statistics, national income and expenditures, taxes, price supports and programs. We must see them from an ecological point of view involved with such inherent needs as freedom, human dignity and happiness. We must recognize the human necessity of keeping physical contact with the land, knowing now and in the generations to come the meaning of the old simplicities and satisfactions.

– "Discussion of Luther Gulick's *Urban Growth and Natural Resources*," undated manuscript, ca 1958

Talk of spiritual values still does not take equal place with the concrete evidence of an expanding economy.

– "The Wilderness Concept," *Ames Forester,*
1962 annual

The great task today of all interested in the preservation of natural areas is to justify them in the eyes of a people the majority of whom are still convinced that nothing should interfere with the grinding progress of our mechanical age.

– "The Wilderness Concept," *Ames Forester,*
1962 annual

We will try to talk about wilderness values, and how they make people feel, and how unhappy we will be without them. Then they will look at you and realize that you must have spent your life in the woods, because you don't really know the facts, and you don't know what makes the country go. They will tell you it was a very fine statement you made but in fact it didn't mean a thing!

– From interview ca 1970s, in Dyan Zaslowsky,
These American Lands (New York: Henry Holt, 1986), 225

Wilderness Management

Wilderness is a delicate adjustment, one which can be disarranged very quickly, and when in addition to its original primitive value it has bound up irretrievably with it a romantic human history, then it becomes doubly imperative that the utmost care be taken in its administration for fear of disturbing values which can never be replaced.

– "The Romance of Portages," *Minnesota Conservationist,*
April 1936

We have all seen what happens when the government does not have control of strategic areas. When private lands enter in, we have uncontrolled logging, uncontrolled resort development, uncontrolled everything and no protection for the adjacent areas because of the contaminating influence of disruption close by.

– Letter to George Laing, December 6, 1941

The basic philosophy behind federal ownership is that only the government can give continuity and stability to natural resource management on these remaining public lands. While it can persuade, cajole and try to educate private owners, it cannot interfere too seriously with their prerogatives as to the property they own. When we consider such benefits as watershed protection, production of wildlife, growing of timber, preservation and proper use of scenic resources, development and maintenance of recreational opportunities, management of soils and grasslands, storage of minerals for the future, we realize that only a federal government can afford to operate on such a long-term, non-profit basis, if the people as a whole are to be served.

– "Our Public Lands: Shall the Public Abdicate Control?"
speech given at the North American Wildlife Conference,
St. Louis, Missouri, March 1958

Wilderness is more than lakes, rivers, and timber along the shores, more than fishing or just camping. It is the sense of the primeval, of space, solitude, silence, and the eternal mystery. It is a fragile quality and is destroyed by man and his machines.

– "Wilderness Preservation," *Naturalist*, Winter 1964

No one likes regulation, but regulation is mandatory when large numbers of people use any area.

– "Wilderness Canoe Country: Minnesota's Greatest
Recreational Asset," *Naturalist*, Spring 1967

The slogan of "Saving Our Wilderness through Multiple Use" is sound only in the proper application of the concept, but is *absolutely erroneous* if it means the kind of management and utilization allowed in the rest of the forest. The wilderness was here long before white men came, needs no logging or mechanized use to survive, only protection. Those who believe that through a continuation of timber harvesting and other adverse uses the wilderness can be saved violate the true concept of zoning.

– "Wilderness Canoe Country: Minnesota's Greatest
Recreational Asset," *Naturalist*, Spring 1967

In our present headlong destruction of all places of natural beauty, both large and small, we can no longer afford to quibble and argue, but should bend all our

efforts toward saving wilderness wherever it is and no
matter what its size or designation.

– "What Is Wilderness?" *Living Wilderness,* Spring 1968

Logging

True wilderness does not permit any halfway measures.
An area is wilderness or it is not and there is no room
for development except of the most primitive type.
Selective logging, with its inevitable construction of
camps and roadways, violates this principle, no matter
how scientific the auspices. Timber stand improvement
as well as artificiality in the treatment of trails, portages
and campsites come under the same category.

– "Wilderness Areas," *Sports Afield,* August 1938

I bring up there the matter of public control over
private logging. That may sound like a pipe dream
now, but someday it will be here and it can't come too
soon to suit me. They can howl all they wish about
regimentation and loss of rights, but the fact remains
that trees belong to everyone and should be handled
like any other public resource of great value, that is
with care and consideration and a certain amount of
good sense.

– Letter to George Laing, December 6, 1941

The old destructive "cut out and get out" philosophy
of those days is still very much alive in our thinking, so
that it is not surprising to find many who even now
view the few wilderness regions we have set aside as
a challenge to move in and make a fortune in spite of
the outraged sentiment of those who do see their
value.

We see these interests constantly at work backed by powerful lobbies, interests which call for the cutting of the last stands of virgin timber, the exploitation of the last untouched reserves of the continent. They make the preservation of any section of wild country a constant battle, and place the comparatively small reservations we have set aside in constant jeopardy.

– "We Need Wilderness," *National Parks Magazine*,
  January–March 1946

To me as an ecologist, it is not true wilderness if it is crisscrossed with logging roads with only a fringe of trees along the lakeshores. Scientifically as well as aesthetically, such interference in the name of harvest and management changes the entire concept of unchanged ancient wilderness.

– "Wilderness Preservation," *Naturalist*, Winter 1964

Planes and Motorboats

[By flying in] I had failed to work for the joy of knowing wilderness. Last time, this was the climax of five full days of woods travel, many portages, many tribulations, miles of bucking the wind. Now I knew. It had come too easy, there must be effort in order to achieve real satisfaction. . . . I had been in the wilderness but . . . was not really of it. It had slipped by me and I had lost the meaning, the real value of it.

– Journal, September 3, 1940

The airplane and the wilderness are in direct conflict and always will be. Wilderness means remoteness and solitude. The airplane eliminates them both.

– "Airplanes to Wilderness," *Living Wilderness*, Spring 1953

As to airplanes, I believe an airspace [reservation] similar to ours [over the Boundary Waters Canoe Area] would be in order for all national parks but especially in air-minded Alaska. One airplane can do more to destroy wilderness atmosphere than a hundred cars; one swoop over a game area can wipe out instantly any feeling of wilderness for a long time.

– Letter to Adolph Murie, September 6, 1960

By the time we were back on deck, the *Radium Gilbert* was moving down the channel and heading up the coast. What a change from riding frail canoes! The headlands of the Bay, while still overpowering, had lost something of their menace, for now we were warm and safe, and in full control once more. Strange, I thought, what the consciousness of steel and power can do to a man's perspective.

– *Runes of the North*, 219

I believe mechanical equipment of all kinds should be kept out of the wilderness, for it is foreign to silence. . . . Silence is one of the most important parts of a wilderness experience; without it the land is nothing more than rocks, trees, and water.

– *Reflections from the North Country*, 40–41

Saving the Pieces

This chapter begins with Sigurd Olson's views about conservation—what conservation is, why it is significant, and its prerequisites, the most essential of which is love. Then we look at his perspective on advocacy. In his earlier years he was not always diplomatic in his efforts to preserve wilderness, but he eventually realized that one can hold true to ideals without being an ideologue and grew frustrated with colleagues who took either a "no-holds-barred" or a legalistic approach to activism.

The third section, on wolves, shows his dramatic change from a wolf hater to an advocate for their preservation. The transformation took place at the University of Illinois in 1931–32, where he earned a master's degree in zoology under the nation's top animal ecologist Victor Shelford. Olson's thesis was the first scientific study of the wolf, and it countered the key stereotypes. From then on, he saw the wolf as both ecologically and symbolically necessary to the wilderness.

He became vice president of the National Parks Association in 1951 and served as president from 1953 to 1959. From 1959 to 1966 he served on the National Park Service's advisory board and as a paid consultant to the Park Service and the Interior Department. As a consultant, he played a role in the establishment of a number of national parks, seashores, historic sites, and wild rivers, from Cape Cod in the east to Point Reyes in the west, from Padre Island in the south to Voyageurs in the north. He was extremely popular among Park Service employees for the motivating talks he gave and for his sympathy for the people working in the field. The quotations chosen for this section reflect his views on the importance of the parks, his work on their behalf, and his motivational talks to Park Service employees.

The last section is devoted to his beloved Quetico–Superior canoe country wilderness. He began fighting to preserve it almost on his arrival there in 1923, when he and his wife, Elizabeth, moved to Ely, and for nearly sixty years he kept up his efforts. His successful role in leading the fight to ban airplanes from the canoe country after World War II gained him prominence in conservation circles in both the United States and Canada and made possible his leadership roles in the National Parks Association and the Wilderness Society. The canoe country was a political battleground that often set precedents for wilderness in other places, and for several decades Olson was both the leading general and diplomat.

Conservation

[When analyzing] resource conservation for recreation and wildlife needs or any other facet of the program before us, it is well to remember that the basic resource we are conserving is the human spirit and the potential happiness of a people.

> – "Resource Conservation for Recreation and Wildlife Needs,"
> at a conference of the Soil Conservation Society of America,
> Asheville, North Carolina, October 21, 1958

To explain why anyone is a conservationist and what motivates him to the point where absorption in the preservation of an environment becomes a personal philosophy means going back to the very beginning of his involvement with the natural scene. I believe one of the basic tenets for anyone really concerned is to have a love for the land, which comes through a long intimacy with natural beauty and living things, an association that breeds genuine affection and has an inherent understanding for its infinite and varied ecology.

– *Open Horizons*, 193–94

Only if there is understanding can there be reverence, and only where there is deep emotional feeling is anyone willing to do battle.

– *Open Horizons*, 194

The ultimate question is what kind of a world do we want, involving man's whole relationship to the earth, what he does to it and how he feels about what he has done. It implies a sense of responsibility when he destroys or befouls his living place, a feeling of having sinned against man's right to enjoy the earth, that he is ethically and morally wrong. Most Americans do not know the real meaning of conservation, think it has only to do with hunting and fishing, roadside beautification, planting trees, and saving places for picnics and camping. Though these are component parts, conservation involves man's attitude in an age where the one ideal seems to be material progress and unlimited utilization of natural resources. Many ignore the fact that preservation of environment is the greatest challenge of our time, and if we fail to meet it in our obsession with a spiraling gross national product, we will lose our cherished freedoms and the richness and beauty our homeland once knew. We need to wonder about the purpose of man and what constitutes the good society. We must face the ecologic crisis aware that man no longer lives with nature as other creatures but has placed himself above and beyond its control.

– *Open Horizons,* 219–20

Without love of the land, conservation lacks meaning or purpose, for only in a deep and inherent feeling for the land can there be dedication in preserving it. Love has many meanings, and it is harder to speak of with respect to environment than of one's attachment to another person. However it is interpreted, love is the lodestone that makes possible the sacrifice of time, energy, and money required to carry on any effort to save a portion of the natural scene or the earth itself from the impact of man's manipulations.

– *Reflections from the North Country,* 125

In a lifetime of trying to preserve wilderness, I have seen love's impact and known its power. Those who oppose destruction or unwise exploitation are accused of being sentimental and impractical. Standing forests have been called "cellulose cemeteries" by those who would destroy them; the fighters have been dubbed the "daffodil fringe of conservation." After a hike along the coast of Olympic National Park to demonstrate the tragedy of building a highway down its length, we were met with an enormous banner across the end of the trail near the little Indian village of La Push: "BIRD WATCHERS GO HOME." We had spent five glorious days along that coast, watched the waves breaking against the pinnacled stacks out from shore, studied the tidal pools with their color and myriad forms of life, climbed the cliffs of points being cut off by the incoming tides from the open sea, had seen what a highway from Lake Ozette in the north would do to this last magnificent stretch of shore. "BIRD WATCHERS GO HOME." As I looked at that banner, I thought how little the opposition really knew of what the good life entailed, and what the shore of magnificent rocks and the rolling Pacific surf really meant. The fact that we won our battle is proof of the power of love, the dedication that went with it, and its growing influence in the world, especially in the young of America who have caught the vision since Earth Day a few years ago.

– *Reflections from the North Country*, 127–28

Advocacy

The swiftest way to nullify our effectiveness is to become known as a group of fanatical gadflies.

– Letter to William Wharton, January 26, 1953

Final victory always goes to those who keep fighting for a worthwhile ideal in spite of reverses.

– Letter to Wilhelmine LaBudde, November 4, 1954

I have found that only when it is possible to sit down with individuals and talk things out can progress be made over a long period of time. There do come times when diplomacy must be thrown out the window, but only when all else has failed. When a shooting war starts then it is anyone's guess as to the outcome.

– Letter to Devereux Butcher, January 30, 1955

Local groups like to feel they are part of the big picture, would like to have a hand in the development of ideas, resent bitterly coming in the back door.

– Letter to Howard Zahniser, September 27, 1957

We have always stood for open discussion and truth. If what we do cannot stand the light of day, something is wrong.

> – Letter to William Wharton, ca October 1958

Without humanity, basic courtesy, and a willingness to see the viewpoints of others any accomplishment is impossible.

> Letter to Ira Gabrielson, April 28, 1960

We strangle ourselves with words, make mountains out of molehills, exchange simplicity for complexity. God save us.

> – Note passed to Jim Marshall during Wilderness Society board meeting, October 1972

One cannot run from a challenge without losing. To flee is signing a death warrant to dignity and character, and, having run, there is no return; one is a weakling forever. Meeting a challenge, though one may be defeated, gives strength, character, and a certain assurance that regardless of outcome, one will survive or go down fighting.

> – *Reflections from the North Country*, 96

There is a different kind of courage, too, that of conviction and belief, the willingness to stand up and be counted before one's enemies. If one has it and fails to face ridicule when the battle lines are drawn, then one is a coward. It is as courageous to take criticism and scorn with equanimity as to withstand a physical threat.

> – *Reflections from the North Country*, 98

Wolves

This was but a phase of the warfare between the predatory animal control and the hosts of gray marauders which each year descend from the wilds of Ontario to prey upon the herds of moose and deer across the border.

– "The Poison Trail," *Sports Afield*, December 1930

Broad across the head and back and heavily furred, he was as savage a looking brute as one could imagine. Such jaws and teeth, it was little wonder that they could ham-string moose or deer and drag them down.

– "The Poison Trail," *Sports Afield*, December 1930

What we most feared, had happened. Only the fat of the entrails had been eaten. They were already killing for fun.

– "The Poison Trail," *Sports Afield*, December 1930

"Yes," I answered, "and I wouldn't be surprised if they've started their murdering already."

– "The Poison Trail," *Sports Afield*, December 1930

Wolves will kill for just the joy of killing and occasionally will eat a small amount returning however for feeding later on.

– Notes for master's thesis, ca December 1930

Judging by the buck we saw today there is a great deal of wasteful killing going on.

– Notes for master's thesis, December 6, 1930

The timber wolf of the north . . . is without doubt the greatest destroyer of big game in this area. The usual range is in the virgin timber and cut over areas of the lake country. The Superior State Game Refuge adjacent as it is to the Canadian Border is fed by bands drifting down from the Ontario Wilds. Trapping of these large predators is of questionable worth for this very reason. For every wolf trapped there might come down dozens in a night from the north. It is doubtful if ever the trapping or poisoning of these animals is worthwhile until some artificial obstruction prevents their coming over.

– Notes for master's thesis, ca December 1930

The public, always gullible, has accepted the most exaggerated reports as to the activities of these animals. If a government ranger or hunter makes a report that timber wolves kill a deer a week, it is accepted as fact and immediately any program which will tend to eliminate the terrible menace to wild life is heartily endorsed. If a statement comes out that a mountain lion has killed an elk, or coyote a sheep, it is without further evidence concluded that all mountain lions are elk killers, and all coyotes live upon are sheep. . . . We are all familiar with similar instances and because there has been no attempt to disprove these theories, no money expended in honest scientific endeavor to find out what is the truth, the campaigns of extermination have been going on unchecked.

– Master's thesis, June 1932

Their depredations have been grossly overestimated.

– Master's thesis, June 1932

The fact that a pack of timber wolves will kill several deer in a night, leaving them where they fell without touching their carcasses is a storage act pure and simple, and not done for the joy of killing as many would make believe.

– Master's thesis, June 1932

During the past quarter of a century, the American people have heard much in regard to the conservation of animal life, but stress has been largely placed on the saving and protection of herbivores at the expense of predatory forms. The predators, those animals which live perforce upon the herbivores, have not as a rule come under the plan of conservation as outlined, and in many areas attempts have been made to eliminate them entirely with total disregard for the influence these forms might have upon the balance of life in the communities of which they are a part.

– "A Study in Predatory Relationship with Particular Reference to the Wolf," *Scientific Monthly*, April 1938

To go into a region where the large carnivores are gone, to see hoofed game with its natural alertness lacking, to know above all that the primitive population has been tampered with, is like traveling through a cultivated estate. Wilderness in all its forms is what the true observer wants to see and with this realization dawns a new appreciation of carnivores and the role they play.

– "A Study in Predatory Relationship with Particular Reference to the Wolf," *Scientific Monthly*, April 1938

It is therefore the purpose of this paper to bring out a few outstanding facts regarding the life habits of one of the largest and most maligned of the predators, the timber wolf of the north (*Canis nubilus* Say), in the hope that some day accumulating evidence may grant it the protection and sanctuary which other forms of life now enjoy. I shall also contend that a large wilderness area may harbor a carnivore population without danger of annihilation to hoofed game and that the constant presence of such large animals of prey as the timber wolf may actually prove of benefit to the herd.

– "A Study in Predatory Relationship with Particular Reference to the Wolf," *Scientific Monthly,* April 1938

The timber wolf is an integral part of the wilderness community, the destruction of which would destroy the fine balance between related forms. To eliminate as vital a relationship as exists between predatory forms and the animals they prey upon, to destroy a mutual dependence, means that artificiality has entered the wilderness picture.

– "A Study in Predatory Relationship with Particular Reference to the Wolf," *Scientific Monthly,* April 1938

At last I caught what I was listening for—the long-drawn quavering howl from over the hills, a sound as wild and indigenous to the north as the muskegs or the northern lights. That was wilderness music, something as free and untamed as there is on this earth.

– *The Singing Wilderness,* 244

We still do not realize that today we can enjoy the wilderness without fear, still do not appreciate the part that predators play in the balanced ecology of any natural community. We seem to prefer herds of semi-domesticated deer and elk and moose, swarms of small game with their natural alertness gone. It is as though we were interested in conserving only a meat supply and nothing of the semblance of the wild.

– *The Singing Wilderness,* 244–45

Wolves are vital and necessary influents in the wilderness, and if removed can change a situation that has been in the making for centuries. If they are taken from the Quetico–Superior, the land will lose some of its character. It will still be a wilderness, but one with the savor and uniqueness gone.

– *Open Horizons*, 169–70

All predators, large or small, beautiful or ugly, have a role to play in keeping the world free from the stench of death and corruption. They are part of the great cycle of interdependence of all forms of life.

– *Of Time and Place*, 89

National Parks

We spend millions of dollars to protect and exhibit man-made works of art. We guard these treasures and would not presume to improve upon them. We hang old masterpieces in exactly the right light, and are hushed and reverent before them. We listen to the world's best symphonies with awe and delight. No one would dream of retouching a Rembrandt or revising a score of Beethoven. Those things are sacred and toward them we have profound respect.

We fail to see our parks as equally sacred and magnificent, that in them we have paintings on a continental scale, museums that cannot be approached by anything conceived by man, majestic symphonies that no one can ever record. These are our greatest masterpieces of all. They are capable of stirring grander emotions, and contributing more to national character

and happiness than anything we have been able to save
of our past.

– "The Challenge of Our National Parks,"
National Parks Magazine, April–June 1954

I hope I shall live long enough to throw the concessions
outside the park boundaries where they belong and
that applies to all of the honky-tonk winter and
summer resort atmosphere for which they have been
responsible. We may never see it but by hard work we
can pave the way. It may take a hundred years to clean
up the parks even though a Congressional Act made it
mandatory that all improper developments be
excluded.

– Letter to Devereux Butcher, December 29, 1954

The concessions have held the whip hand over the park
service for so long that the present administration as
well as those in the past have been unable to do much
about it.

– Letter to Max Gilstrup, January 15, 1956

I feel there is not enough clarity of firmness in
Washington or in the local staffs regarding such
developments. What is needed is a firm, crystal clear
policy and less of the tolerance exhibited toward
local views.

– Letter to Max Gilstrup, January 15, 1956

Most of our national parks are in the far West, and in
spite of high annual visitation there will always be
millions who cannot visit them. . . . What people need
in an expanding industrial complex such as ours are
areas close enough to be lived with and enjoyed
without great expenditure of time or money. It is not

enough to see them once a year. They should become part of people's lives. Their very existence close to urban areas would exert a stabilizing and enriching influence.

– "Cape Cod National Park," report for National
Park Service, March 1958

Potential National Park Service areas must not be considered in the light of the present but over a long period of time. In surveying new possibilities we can no longer afford to think in terms of Yellowstones, Yosemites, or Glaciers. With very few exceptions, such primeval opportunities are gone. We must acquire now what we can of the remnants, making allowances for changes that have taken place, looking to the future to heal the scars of exploitation and neglect, hoping that eventually the ideal may be reached. Unless we do this, we must abandon any thought of including many still important areas which in time could justify acquisition.

– "Cumberland Island," report for National
Park Service, March 1958

The many millions who drive through our national parks and forests, though they may never set foot on any of the back-country trails, never know the wilderness except from their automobiles, nevertheless are conscious of its power, a realization that gives significance to everything they see. The lure is more than scenery, varied vistas and magnificent lookout points; it is the consciousness of being at the threshold of the unknown.

– *Listening Point*, 239–40

I believe the time has come to bring into the system actual National Park Areas in the Middle West and the

East. To be sure the standards will not be the same as the original primeval parks of the west, nor will they be as large, but there are many beautiful areas that can be brought back to primeval significance with protection. There are many places in New England now growing up to forests that would fill a great need. Remnant shopping is what [former National Park Service Director] Connie [Wirth] called it but this remnant shopping might someday provide superlative national parks. . . .

. . . The American public has come to believe that magnificence is to be expected in any national park and this has been true. With few truly magnificent areas left except the North Cascades we will have to change our perspective and point of view. To me a fine stretch of tundra is magnificent so is a northern lake, or a swamp, or an isolated stretch of lake or seashore, or an island. You don't have to have the gigantic. It is all in the eye and the mind of the seer.

– Letter to National Park Service Director
  George Hartzog, May 12, 1966

No matter what you are called, no matter what political pressures are brought to bear on you every time a new development is proposed, look at it carefully and don't be too tolerant. Give in, if you have to, but only as a last resort. What you have is a sacred trust, a trust that future generations will hold you accountable for. Let's not look ahead just the next ten years with a definite use graph. Let's give it the broad long vision. Let's think of a hundred years, five hundred years, a thousand years, and with all of the planning that you do, do not be shortsighted. Do not lean toward immediacy. Look ahead and plan for the future. Look ahead to a time when our people will be clamoring for these areas as they have never clamored before. Look ahead to the time when, due to the Service itself and its ideals, these places will remain intact.

– Remarks to National Park Service master plan
  team members, ca mid-1960s

Quetico–Superior Wilderness

You can't touch that country without taking something away from it that can never be replaced. . . . The only salvation of the country on both sides of the boundary is to make an international park out of it which would lie absolutely inviolate, a wilderness preserve for all time. . . . the only salvation of our border country is to make it a wilderness park set aside for all time as a recreation area not to be touched by a development mad public.

– Letter to Ernest Oberholtzer, January 28, 1931

I firmly believe that the day is not far distant when the shadow of the logger's axe will no longer hang over the most picturesque areas of the north, when the people will demand that it be left inviolate.

– From draft of a speech, ca 1934

If the present rate of road building and improvement goes on, it is safe to predict that in ten years, there will be no part of the Superior which cannot be reached by automobile, and though the country will be filled with resorts and private homes, its present charm will be gone, for it will no longer be a wilderness, merely another of many vacation lands. Now it is different and

has an individuality all its own. Open it up with a road
to every lake and building site and it will be just like all
the rest of the country.

– "Roads or Planes in the Superior,"
Minnesota Waltonian, April 1934

Here is a wilderness lake country of unequalled beauty
and charm, thousands of lakes and streams intimately
connected and interlaced, a paradise for the wilderness
traveler.

– "A New Policy Needed for the Superior,"
Minnesota Conservationist, May 1934

Ask any one of the thousands of visitors who have come
to the Superior during the last few years what is it
about the country which appeals to him most, and he
will invariably answer that it is not the fish and not the
scenery, superb as it may be, but the fact that here is one
spot where he can get away from crowds and enjoy
primitive wilderness conditions.

– "A New Policy Needed for the Superior,"
Minnesota Conservationist, May 1934

The day is fast coming when the trees in the Superior,
particularly along the canoe routes, will be worth far
more as integral parts of the lakeland wilderness than
as board feet of timber on the skids, when water
flowing over a natural rapids or falls will in just that
way be fulfilling its highest possible use, rather than
turning the wheels of industry. This demand is
growing, and sooner or later will make itself heard.

– "The Preservation of Wilderness Areas,"
unpublished speech, ca 1935

I shall always maintain that a true wilderness never can be tampered with or improved if it is to retain its character and that applies even within absolutely restricted areas to portage and camp site improvement beyond the bounds of bare necessity. The idea of multiple use can work splendidly in some parts of the Superior, but not where it touches vitally country that some day and not in the very far future is destined to have as its "highest use" recreation and that solely.

– Letter to Ray Harmon, April 9, 1935

Good canoeing waters demand shorelines that are preferably irregular, and above all, lakes that are narrow and split up by islands and bays into a labyrinth of channels and passageways. This is exactly the condition we find in the border country.

– "The Evolution of a Canoe Country,"
Minnesota Conservationist, May 1935

We must weigh the issues well before we allow the ogre of development and the false ideal of multiple use to rob us of something which seems so particularly suited to the needs of those who want to leave the beaten trails; those who love the swish of paddle and the song of running water. For these the country was created, and for them it should be kept, unspoiled and unchanged as it has come down to us through the centuries.

– "The Evolution of a Canoe Country,"
Minnesota Conservationist, May 1935

More than anything else in the world, I would like to see what is left of the canoe country given the protection of Wilderness Area status.

– Letter to Ken Reid, November 20, 1939

Now in 1948, the lines are clearly drawn and the outcome will determine for all time whether or not America will have a wilderness canoe country.

– "Let's Finish What We Started," *Outdoor America,*
February 1948

In short, if anything happens to these two bills, America must bid farewell to its Superior Roadless Area and admit that she cannot afford the luxury of preserving this last small fragment of wilderness canoe country she has left.

– "Let's Finish What We Started," *Outdoor America,*
February 1948

It was bad enough that Crooked Lake itself was ruined, but the two resorts soon spread their activities like cancerous growths into the hitherto untouched tributary lakes to the north and south, planted boats all over the adjacent Quetico, destroyed campsites and littered them with their refuse. They appropriated for their own hundreds of square miles of wilderness and destroyed them as effectively for primitive enjoyment as though they had cut huge sections off the map.

– "Let's Finish What We Started," *Outdoor America,*
February 1948

Unless these private lands are absorbed by the government immediately, unless resort developments already begun are purchased, the old wilderness as we knew it before the war is doomed.

– "Let's Finish What We Started," *Outdoor America,*
February 1948

I feel personally that it would not be too much to consider setting aside some of the interior lakes for canoe use only, allowing the use as now of motors on the larger waters adjacent to the resort areas.

– Talk before the Lutheran Men's Club of Ely, Minnesota, August 20, 1957

We are not living in the same era when the first controversies arose over this area. Trees do not mean the same. They have different values when they are part of an ancient ecology of great social value. The people of the future with wild country rapidly disappearing everywhere will be looking not for a partial or managed wilderness, but for the real thing.

– "Wilderness Preservation," *Naturalist*, Winter 1964

Personally I feel that mechanized use should eventually be taken out of any wilderness, but am practical enough to realize that any such regulation must be done through cooperation with the State of Minnesota as well as the interests bordering the area and the needs of local communities. This will take study and research for the problems are great and involved.

– "Wilderness Preservation," *Naturalist*, Winter 1964

The old concept to me is permitting logging in the face of a growing mass use which makes it untenable. People today . . . are not willing to wait for the country to come back. Those who see these last pockets of red and white pine or even stands of spruce and jack feel they are as precious as museum pieces of the past and as worthy of cherishing and protecting as famous paintings.

– Letter to Frank Hubachek, July 11, 1964

Greater use, however, brings its own hazards to the wilderness, especially when it means mechanization in the form of outboard motors, snowmobiles, and other craft or vehicles. It is my firm belief that mechanized use of any kind in this small area is destructive of wilderness values and that it should be strictly regulated and in time eliminated entirely.

– "Wilderness Canoe Country: Minnesota's Greatest
Recreational Asset," *Naturalist*, Spring 1967

Correctly interpreted, the idea of *zoning the canoe country for wilderness use* and relegating all other uses to the major part of the forest is the only hope for the Boundary Waters Canoe Area.

– "Wilderness Canoe Country: Minnesota's Greatest
Recreational Asset," *Naturalist*, Spring 1967

Must we repeat over and over the ghastly mistakes of the past, desecrating the landscape, destroying its wildlife, poisoning its clear waters, and leaving scars that will take thousands of years to heal?

– "Wilderness Challenge," *Living Wilderness*, Summer 1970

You must understand that, in saving the Boundary Waters Canoe Area, in saving any wilderness area, you are saving more than rocks and trees and mountains and lakes and rivers. What you are really saving is the human spirit. What you are really saving is the human soul.

– Quoted in George Vukelich, "Sigurd Olson:
What You Are Really Saving Is the Human Soul,"
Ely (Minn.) Miner, July 27, 1977

LANDSCAPE OF
THE UNIVERSE

The phrase "landscape of the universe" was originally used by the philosopher Josef Pieper in a discussion about St. Thomas Aquinas's theology. Sigurd Olson later used it as the title of the final chapter of *Open Horizons*. In this chapter we look at three broad themes: the land ethic, the land aesthetic, and his thoughts on theology and philosophy. The "land ethic," a term created by Aldo Leopold (a founder of the Wilderness Society and author of the classic *A Sand County Almanac*), reflects a holistic, ecological worldview. Just as certain norms of behavior are required to build and maintain a healthy society, so are they required to maintain a healthy environment on which society depends. As Leopold put it in an often-quoted maxim: "A thing is right when it tends to preserve the integrity, stability, and beauty of the biotic community. It is wrong when it tends otherwise."

The *land aesthetic* is a term created by philosopher J. Baird Callicott to describe a new, in fact revolutionary, perspective on the beauty of nature. The dominant principle in Western culture—conceived, created, distributed, and perpetuated by artists—was based almost entirely on visual beauty. From this came such terms as *landscape* and *scenery*. The national parks, monuments of scenic grandeur, were chosen on this basis. But Leopold and Olson created a new aesthetic that judged the beauty of nature in a far more holistic way, including all the senses.

They also professed that knowledge of evolution deepens our perception of beauty and that an understanding of ecology broadens it. A marsh, for example, does not conform to the convention of the picturesque, but a mind informed by evolutionary and ecological biology and senses steeped in the sounds and smells and tastes of the marsh will perceive it as beautiful and precious. Olson went further than Leopold in incorporating humans into his land aesthetic, asserting that memories of previous experiences with friends and loved ones, as well as knowledge of the human history of a place, deepen one's appreciation for its beauty.

The final selection of quotations looks at the underlying thoughts about God, spirit, and human destiny that drove Olson's search for meaning and provided the theological basis of his wilderness philosophy. In addition to Pieper, he was influenced by such philosophers and theologians as Pierre Teilhard de Chardin, Lewis Mumford, Aldous and Julian Huxley, and Pierre Lecomte du Noüy, all of whom believed that mankind is proceeding along a path of spiritual evolution that will lead toward union with God. Olson combined this thesis, known as evolutionary humanism, with his theory of racial memory, the belief that humans maintain a biological longing for close contact with nature, despite urban life. He knew that the silence and the solitude and the noncivilized surroundings of wilderness provide a physical context in which we can more easily rediscover our inner selves, partly because of the lack of distractions and partly because humans were *designed* for close contact with nature. At the same time, free of distraction and in tune with our natural selves, we can more readily experience the eternal mystery and our own participation in this mystery. Such an experience not only gives meaning to our lives, but leads to the view that all creation is sacred.

Land Ethic

Each camp reflects the spirit of those who have used it last.

– "Wilderness Manners," *Sports Afield*, May 1945

Haven't we a responsibility to pass on to future generations some of the grand heritages which are becoming scarcer and scarcer? Have we of this generation the right to say, "We will put a dam in here and a dam here," and destroy something that people one hundred years from now will view with regret?. . . Should not we use discretion and wonder sometimes whether, in our enthusiasm for altering and reshaping the surface of our continent, we are not destroying things that someday may be without price?

– Department of Interior hearing, Washington, D.C., April 3, 1950

The good citizen knows that the land is a sacred trust. He feels that, when he passes it on to future generations, it must be as good as when he found it, or better.

– "Conservation and Citizenship," *Gopher Historian*, April 1953

Conservation and good citizenship go hand in hand. You cannot have one without the other.

– "Conservation and Citizenship," *Gopher Historian*, April 1953

There can be no real, lasting land ethic without love. Ecology must also include the emotional aspects of mankind's relationship to the universe, as well as ethics.

– Letter to George Laing, June 30, 1955

Let us restore and improve natural habitats in places which have been disturbed, recognizing our relationship to the intricate web of life of all creatures and the basic truth that in doing so we rejuvenate ourselves.

– "What of Beautiful Minnesota?" in *Century 2,* 1972

Man is slowly learning to live in harmony with the earth, using his vast technology to right past wrongs, to clean despoiled rivers and poisoned air. "It has never been man's gift to make wildernesses," Wallace Stegner observed. "But he can make deserts, and has." The choice is ours. I have faith that the wild places will win out.

– "A Longing for Wilderness," in *Wilderness USA,* 1973

Freedom of the wilderness means many things to different people. If you really want to enjoy it, you must recognize your responsibilities as adult humans living in a world with others. No one has a right to kill chipmunks, squirrels, whisky jacks, seagulls, or any other form of life which adds interest to a wilderness campsite. They are a large part of the wilderness enjoyment, as much a part as lichens on the rocks, as trees, shrubs, and mosses, as the vistas of fleets of floating islands in the distance, as the roar of rapids. Such things belong to everyone and must not be disturbed. Freedom gives no one license to change a heritage that belongs to the ages.

– *Reflections from the North Country,* 105

Does it really matter if you clean your fish on the smooth glaciated ledges beside the water, leaving the rotted, maggoty remains to offend others? It may seem utterly silly not to use detergent in your dishwater. But all such practices have an impact on the purity of the water. It is the cumulative habits of many which determine what happens to the environment. You may feel that whatever you do will never be noticed, for the waves will wash your sins away leaving no signs of anyone having been there. You may now have just a slight growing consciousness of guilt about your behavior, a sign perhaps of growing maturity.

– *Of Time and Place,* 168

We must ask ourselves how we truly feel about what we have done to the planet during our brief tenure upon it. Are we really willing to do what we should, and are we mature enough to forget selfish interests? When critical areas are being threatened, will we stand up and fight for them no matter how unpopular such stands might be? Our most important goal is preservation of the land which is our home. We must be eternally vigilant and embrace the broad concept of an environmental ethic to survive.

– *Of Time and Place,* 170

Land Aesthetic

The terrain has a different meaning now, not only through what we shared, but because of what we had known that gave us the feeling of the land itself, its eras of the past, the time when the Canadian Shield came into being, when prehistoric seas laid down formations of Athabasca sandstone, the glacial periods of the last million years when the routes we traveled were shaped by the gouging of the ice, the crossing of Asiatics over Bering Strait and their slow filtration into the south, the days of explorers and *voyageurs,* up to the swiftly changing time of today. All this we had shared and lived over many thousands of miles until almost

unconsciously the long history of the primitive country
we had traversed was absorbed into our minds and
thoughts. We had left no mark on the country itself, but
the land had left its mark on us.

– *Runes of the North,* 167–68

It seemed to me after I had absorbed this concept
my roots went down more deeply, like those of a
black spruce penetrating the tangled mat over a
glacial bog.

– *Open Horizons,* 170–71

The study of the earth and its shaping opened up new
vistas to me, and when finally I was aware of the
intricate relationships of all forms of life in the area, my
understanding grew to the point where I felt more at
home in the wilderness than ever before. The story of
Indians, voyageurs, explorers, and settlers added still
more color and warmth, increased by the personal
associations of guides and woodsmen and the men
I cruised with through the lakes and rivers of the
Quetico–Superior.

– *Open Horizons,* 173

Cultural, esthetic, and intangible values are a composite
of many things: beauty of terrain, geological and
ecological understanding, and the background of
human history. Knowledge of how the land was
formed, its volcanic eras, the vast glacial periods
which smoothed, gouged and shaped its surface into
what we see today is vital to appreciation of its
values. The evolution of wildlife and vegetation, their
slow adjustment to climate, water, soil, and land
forms are as necessary as having an understanding
of the hopes, dreams, and fears of those who lived

and labored here hundreds and even thousands of years ago. All this imparts deeper meaning and even enhances its beauty.

– "The Values of Voyageurs National Park,"
Minnesota Conservationist, May–June 1971

Beauty is composed of many things and never stands alone. It is part of horizons, blue in the distance, great primeval silences, knowledge of all things of the earth. It embodies the hopes and dreams of those who have gone before, including the spirit world; it is so fragile it can be destroyed by a sound or thought. It may be infinitesimally small or encompass the universe itself. It comes in a swift conception wherever nature has not been disturbed.

– *Reflections from the North Country*, 83

God, Spirit, and Human Destiny

All happiness comes from within, all successful living comes from a proper appreciation of spiritual values.

– Untitled speech for a Legion Auxiliary memorial service,
Ely, Minnesota, May 1, 1940

Without the civilizing influence of man, without the warmth of godliness and spirit, the earth is merely a cold and brutish planet.

– Journal, November 6, 1940

Put yourself in harmony with the great life stream, with universal forces, with Christianity if one would be happy. . . . Man is a biological accident, is therefore humble, realizes that to be man capable of love takes away egotism, makes it imperative that he live as Christ

would have him live, that he himself does not count
except as he gives and loves others.

– Journal, January 13, 1947

The human spirit is the highest development of nature,
bigger than the stars, bigger than atoms, bigger than the
laws of the solar system. . . . The spirit of man is the
flowering of nature, greater than any other phenomenon,
greater than the whirling spheres, greater than space,
infinity.

– Journal, January 13, 1947

The grandest search of man is the search for an
understanding of God.

– Journal, January 13, 1947

What is happening now makes it even more important
to keep the flame alive, give people something to hold
to, something to fight for that is bigger than politics,
bigger than the problems the world is constantly facing,
something in the way of a philosophical concept that
lies at the root of any happiness the race can find.

– Letter to Olaus Murie, November 11, 1956

The longer I observe and think and write the surer
I am that God is all that counts. Certainly physical
immortality is a juvenile conception of frightened man.
Only those who align themselves with great minds and
the overall intelligence from which we all come know
the meaning of life and where man is going.

– Letter to Robert Day, December 29, 1959

Back as far as men can go there is evidence of an
intuitive sense of immortality and the presence of a
divine being which may be called God. There is no
proof but all races have it in different forms. It goes far

beyond instinct. When it arose no one knows and no one will ever know. It was there long, long ago and it is the spark that separates man from the beast. His consciousness of a higher power, his wish to identify himself with this power, is what gives man his dignity and in a sense Godliness.

– Journal, February 4, 1960

Man's evolutionary goal is to advance the human spirit and mind to its fullest possibilities.

– Journal, December 28, 1960

You say you are convinced of the truth of reincarnation. I have given this a great deal of thought through my study not only of Christianity but of Buddhism. At one time I traveled with a Buddhist and so felt close to his beliefs. I feel now that reincarnation refers to the spirit, and that our spirits will, without question, live on in others. I am not egotistical enough to believe that my particular spirit will survive intact in any other form, but if some small intimation of its influence survives, that is sufficient immortality for me.

– Letter to Winthrop Steele, February 9, 1962

Granted that creatures other than man show love and feeling not only for their young but for each other, only in man has it progressed to where it is a major force in his development and culture.

– *Runes of the North*, 14

The Sermon on the Mount is enough of a code to live by. That epitomizes all that counts, all evolution of the mind and spirit.

– Journal notes for book manuscript called "The Echo Trail," undated, ca 1965

On one point all agree: that spiritual values contribute to the joy and richness of living; that without them existence lacks color and warmth, and the soul itself is drab and impoverished. We accept the broad premise that such values, inspired by the contemplation of wilderness beauty and mystery, were the well-springs of our dawning culture and the first significant expressions of the human mind.

> – "The Spiritual Need," at the Ninth Wilderness Conference,
> San Francisco, April 1965

I am confident that Stone Age man, who some forty thousand years ago painted his symbols on the caves of France and Spain, was powerfully stirred by the mystery of the unknown and the spirit world that dwelt there. Such surviving examples of prehistoric art tell of the millennia when man pondered his environment as an awareness finally dawned that the dreams, longings, fears, and hopes that haunted him could be translated into forms of meaning and permanence. Symbols from which spells and magic went forth to influence hunting, fertility, and success in his various ventures—they represented the growing world of the spirit, the first indications of the mighty concept of immortality, and the realization that after death men would dwell forever in the vast vault of the heavens. It was then he emerged from the dark abyss of his past into a world of mind and soul and began to give form to his deepest and most profound emotions.

> – "The Spiritual Need," at the Ninth Wilderness Conference,
> San Francisco, April 1965

This much we know is true: that while a man is with his gods, no matter who they may be, he can forget the problems and petty distractions of the workaday world and reach out to spiritual realizations that renew him. Only through receptiveness, contemplation, and awareness does anyone open himself to the great intuitions and consciousness of what life and the universe really mean.

– "The Spiritual Need," at the Ninth Wilderness Conference, San Francisco, April 1965

Over the centuries a host of other great minds have also believed that if through awareness and wonder man might recognize even faintly his personal relationship to the universe, he would then partake and become part of the order and reason that governs his existence, the movement of galaxies, as well as the minutest divisions of matter. From the early scriptures and through all cultures, this profound concept has echoed and reechoed as man realized its immensity and spiritual connotations. A grand concept, it has increased the stature of man and stood the test of time.

– "The Spiritual Need," at the Ninth Wilderness Conference, San Francisco, April 1965

I cannot hold with the idea of absurdity or for that matter existentialism. Life is not absurd nor is a good life lived solely for oneself. Only in the belief that life can be beautiful and have meaning is it worthwhile.

– Letter to Jim Reston, August 23, 1965

I am a firm believer in the thought that what a man believes lives on in whoever has been touched.

– Letter to Edward Wood, September 21, 1965

We must develop a philosophy which considers the great imponderables, the ancient codes of ethics embodying man's sense of oneness and dependence on nature. While technology may redress the wrongs of the past, it is not the answer unless man's spiritual welfare is concerned. We need an ecology of man in harmony with the ecologies of all living things and a recognition of the truth that our search for utopia reflects fundamental human needs.

– *Open Horizons*, 220

Over the centuries a host of perceptive minds have believed that if man saw his relationship to the earth and the universe, he could become part of the order and reason that governs his existence, the movement of the galaxies as well as the minutest divisions of matter, a faculty we of the twentieth century seem to have lost.

– *Open Horizons*, 221

God is spirit and thought. . . . Man's greatest growth is the evolution of mind and spirit and those who recognize this are blessed. To me this is God and it is enough. I no longer try to define God but accept this premise as the final answer.

– Letter to Reverend Robert Gamble, July 4, 1971

We no longer face a physical frontier, but a change in philosophy, a complete reversal of our attitude toward the earth that might open the door to a golden era far more resplendent than the old.

– *Reflections from the North Country*, 5

The struggle for spirit has replaced the physical, and in his evolution psychologically man's greatest minds have become aware of the emptiness of material striving. The struggle has become a positive drive toward perfection, all in keeping with his final hope: realization of the kingdom of God within him.

– Reflections from the North Country, 48

What civilization needs today is a culture of sensitivity and tolerance and an abiding love of all creatures including mankind. The future of man is the development of spirit, with love and gentleness resting in the broad field of the humanities, not in his ability to build. When he deems it his first duty to produce things for his wealth and comfort, with the end being consumption and waste, he loses dignity and purpose.

– Reflections from the North Country, 49

I may have to be content knowing there is some logic and reason behind the framework of the universe.

– Reflections from the North Country, 57

At last I am beginning to believe I am part of all this life and to know how I evolved from the primal dust to a creature capable of seeing beauty. This is compensation enough. No one can ever take this dream away; it will be with me until the day I have seen my last sunset, and listened for a final time to the wind whispering through the pines.

– Reflections from the North Country, 57

I *do believe* . . . that no one can understand the cosmos without first being convinced there is a power behind all things. There is an energy, a thought spectrum, like a Van Allen Belt, in which all ideas and spiritual beliefs surround the earth like the belt of matter surrounding earth. We in our consciousness flow with this mythical thought.

– In Jim Dale Vickery, "A Bluejay Calling," Canoe, *February 1980*

Odds and Ends

War

Young men have always died for their countries and old men have always used wars as excuses for covering up their own problems of unemployment, dissatisfaction, economic difficulties, and always under the guise of fighting for something.

– "Armistice Day 1938," draft of speech, November 9, 1938

Writing of funny little stories, of even serious little stories telling of a man's love of the earth and the wilderness, seems foolish when men are dying and suffering, giving their all, when women and children are being bombed. The only important thing at all is the maintenance of the kind of civilization that we think is worthwhile.

– Journal, February 23, 1940

I told them that the same life that flows in a man's veins flows also in leaves and flowers, that the substance called protoplasm was identical no matter what type of cell sheltered it, that all life was related and possibly started from some central source of creation, that animals, plants of men, Japs, Germans, Chinese or Americans were all driven by the same primordial force, that underneath there was no difference.

– "Seventeen," essay draft ca early 1940s

Killing in the army is an impersonal thing. This civilization of ours has a malignant cancer growing away inside it, a cancer that is as much living tissue as the rest of the body but something that has to be cut out immediately if the body is to survive. That is your job and the millions of other chaps who are over. Your job is to help cut out the infection, and if cutting out the infection means destroying those responsible for it then you should have no more compunction about it than if you were a surgeon cutting out live tissue during an operation. In other words do not let this war become personal to you. It is a cold deadly impersonal business all the way through. In order that men may live happily in the future, live in peace without fear or want, such cancerous growths as Hitler's and Hirohito's philosophy must be destroyed. For beliefs can be as malignant as disease and the only way to destroy the cause is to do away with those who foster and support such beliefs. This is a war against a false philosophy of life, in fact it is a crusade against evil and your generation has been called to fight and cleanse the earth once again. Mankind it seems always has to fight for liberty and the right to happiness.

– Letter to Sigurd T. Olson, ca 1943

We are all of the whole world, no nations, no racial groups, just men, and force is ridiculous and we must sooner or later adopt the Gandhian philosophy of gentleness and nonresistance.

– "Notes for Carleton," speech notes ca early 1960s

I saw the ruin in cities such as Vienna and Berlin, cities with the stench of death still about them. I wondered if the time would ever come [if] they would ever return to the beautiful cities they once had been. I shall always remember the railroad tracks. . . . Germans returning to their homeland to be repatriated after the war [were] arriving in cattle cars and because it was Easter [the cars were] decorated with branches of evergreen. I could see these people filing off the cars and standing on the platform with no place to go and nothing to eat, their eyes round and fearful. These are the memories I carried with me back to my home, memories I would never forget, memories which to this day give me nightmares.

– "My Education in Europe," unpublished manuscript ca 1960s

Your questioning the war in Viet Nam and other issues has been unsettling for you and many others. Young men are asking embarrassing questions about everything. And this to me is good. When I was your age we didn't ask questions. World War I came along to make the world safe for democracy and we all believed it. When World War II came along it was much the same but some of the glamour had worn off. During the past twenty years all of the glamour has gone and now for the first time young men are wondering where it will lead, [they are] thinking young men.

– Letter to Jim Reston, August 23, 1965

Morality and Popular Culture

Magazines have changed. They're becoming obsessed with sex. Past cultures that were obsessed with sex collapsed.

– In Jim Vickery, "Profile of a Pioneer: Sigurd F. Olson," *Backpacking Journal,* Summer 1977

Why don't you bathe? Cut your hair? Why don't you put on clean clothes once in a while? . . . As an ecologist

I look at you as a species doomed to extinction. Cleanliness is absolutely essential for survival. When animals befoul themselves they become diseased, vermin-ridden and die.

> – Words spoken to long-haired environmentalists in San Francisco, late 1960s. Recalled in speech transcript, "The Revolution in Environmental Concern," ca 1969

Love

Don't hate and resent. Life is too short for either. Be tolerant and let love come in with its understanding. The world is made up of many kinds of people, all of them important to the overall pattern.

I understand your wanting to help people. That is the wonder of your type, your sense of mission and unselfish giving. But to help people and to write about them, you must understand them and to understand them you must love them. Love opens the door to everything.

No, you are not alone. There are many who feel as you do and the hope of the world is in the frustration you feel, the wanting to do something about it. But don't adopt the cancerous philosophy of having faith only in yourself.

> – Letter to Adina Lundquist, June 13, 1953

Last Words

A new adventure is coming up, and I'm sure it will be a good one.

> – Found in his typewriter on January 14, 1982, the day after his death

Writings by Sigurd F. Olson

Books

The Singing Wilderness. New York: Alfred A. Knopf, 1956. Reprint, Minneapolis: University of Minnesota Press, 1997.

Listening Point. New York: Alfred A. Knopf, 1958. Reprint, Minneapolis: University of Minnesota Press, 1997.

The Lonely Land. New York: Alfred A. Knopf, 1961. Reprint, Minneapolis: University of Minnesota Press, 1997.

Runes of the North. New York: Alfred A. Knopf, 1963. Reprint, Minneapolis: University of Minnesota Press, 1997.

Open Horizons. New York: Alfred A. Knopf, 1969. Reprint, Minneapolis: University of Minnesota Press, 1998.

The Hidden Forest. New York: Viking Press, 1969.

Wilderness Days. New York: Alfred A. Knopf, 1972.

Reflections from the North Country. New York: Alfred A. Knopf, 1976. Reprint, Minneapolis: University of Minnesota Press, 1998.

Of Time and Place. New York: Alfred A. Knopf, 1982. Reprint, Minneapolis: University of Minnesota Press, 1998.

Songs of the North. Edited by Howard Frank Mosher. Penguin Nature Library. New York: Penguin Books, 1987.

The Collected Works of Sigurd F. Olson: The Early Writings, 1921–1934. Edited by Mike Link. Introduction by Robert Keith Olson. Stillwater, Minn.: Voyageur Press, 1988.

The Collected Works of Sigurd F. Olson: The College Years, 1935–1944. Edited by Mike Link. Introduction by Jim Klobuchar. Stillwater, Minn.: Voyageur Press, 1990.

The Meaning of Wilderness: Essential Articles and Speeches. Edited and with an introduction by David Backes. Minneapolis, Minn.: University of Minnesota Press, 2001.

Articles and Book Chapters

This section lists Olson's magazine and newspaper articles and book chapters, arranged in chronological order. Speeches that were revised for publication are included in this section. (Speeches published in conference proceedings follow in a separate section.) The following are not included: book excerpts, published letters to the editor, or titles of Olson's "America Out of Doors" syndicated newspaper column, which was published in a few American newspapers between 1941 and 1944.

1920s

"Canoe Tourist Finds Joys of the Great Outdoors through the Vast Watered Wilderness of the North." *Milwaukee Journal*, July 31, 1921. (This article also was printed about the same time in the *Nashwauk (Minn.) Herald* under the title "Describes Cruise thru the Woods," and indeed may have appeared there first. The Olson family found a clipping of the article in 1999; it is undated, but the issue number of 28 appears, indicating a likely mid-July timeframe. Sigurd would have been somewhat disappointed, however, because there was no byline. The *Milwaukee Journal* article is the first to list his name as the writer.)

"Fishin' Jewelry." *Field and Stream*, November 1927.

"Snow Wings." *Boys' Life*, March 1928.

"Reflections of a Guide." *Field and Stream*, June 1928. In *The Meaning of Wilderness*, 3–13.

1930s

"Duck Heaven." *Outdoor Life*, October 1930.

"Confessions of a Duck Hunter." *Sports Afield*, October 1930.

"Stag Pants Galahads." *Sports Afield*, November 1930.

"The Poison Trail." *Sports Afield*, December 1930.

"Spring Fever." *Sports Afield*, April 1931.

"The Blue-Bills Are Coming!" *Sports Afield*, October 1931.

"Papette." *Sports Afield*, January–February 1932.

"Search for the Wild." *Sports Afield*, May–June 1932. In *The Meaning of Wilderness*, 14–21.

"Fortune at Lac La Croix." *Sports Afield*, September–October 1932.

"Trail's End." *Sports Afield*, October 1933.

"Roads or Planes in the Superior." *Minnesota Waltonian*, April 1934.

"A New Policy Needed for the Superior." *Minnesota Conservationist*, May 1934.

"Cruising in the Arrowhead." *Outdoors*, May 1934.

"The Evolution of a Canoe Country." *Minnesota Conservationist*, May 1935.

"Sere, Climax, and Influent Animals with Special Reference to the Transcontinental Coniferous Forest of North America." Coauthored with Victor E. Shelford. *Ecology*, July 1935.

"The Romance of Portages." *Minnesota Conservationist*, April 1936. In *The Meaning of Wilderness*, 22–28.

"Let's Go Exploring." *Field and Stream*, June 1937. In *The Meaning of Wilderness*, 29–38.

"Organization and Range of the Pack." *Ecology*, January 1938.

"Taking Us, Dad?" *Field and Stream*, January 1938.

"A Study in Predatory Relationship with Particular Reference to the Wolf." *Scientific Monthly*, April 1938.

"Wilderness Areas." *Sports Afield*, August 1938.

"Why Wilderness?" *American Forests*, September 1938. In *The Meaning of Wilderness*, 39–47.

"Mallards Are Different." *Field and Stream*, November 1938.

"The Immortals of Argo." *Sports Afield*, July 1939.

"Mallards of Back Bay." *Sports Afield*, October 1939.

1940s

"Fireside Pictures." *Field and Stream*, March 1940.

"The Last Mallard." *Sports Afield*, November 1940.

"What! No Bass?" *Field and Stream*, January 1941.

"The Bohemians." *Minneapolis Star-Journal*, March 23, 1941.

"First Spring Flower." *Minneapolis Star-Journal*, March 30, 1941.

"Easter on the Prairie." *Minneapolis Star-Journal*, April 13, 1941.

"Spring Morning." *Minneapolis Star-Journal*, April 20, 1941.

"The Iron Mine." *Minneapolis Star-Journal*, April 27, 1941.

"Balm of Gilead." *Minneapolis Star-Journal*, May 4, 1941.

"Opening Day." *Minneapolis Star-Journal*, May 11, 1941.

"The Three Spruces." *Minneapolis Star-Journal*, May 18, 1941.

"Prairie Pool." *Minneapolis Star-Journal*, May 25, 1941.

"Swan Song." *Minneapolis Star-Journal*, June 1, 1941.

"The Call of the Flock." *Minneapolis Star-Journal*, June 8, 1941.

"Wilderness Short Cuts." *Sports Afield*, 1942 fishing annual.

"War Comes to the Quetico." *Sports Afield*, February 1942.

"Wilderness Again on Trial." *Outdoor America*, May–June 1942.

"Quetico–Superior Wilderness International and Unique." *Living Wilderness*, December 1942.

"Packs and Paddles." *Sports Afield*, 1943 fishing annual.

"Gold in Them Hills." *Sports Afield*, July 1944.

"The Spring Hole." *Outdoor Life*, September 1944.

"I'm a Jump Shooter." *Sports Afield*, October 1944.

"Shift of the Wind." *Sports Afield*, December 1944.

"Wilderness Manners." *Sports Afield*, May 1945.

"The Purist." *Conservation Volunteer*, May–June 1945.

"Flying In." *Sports Afield*, September 1945. In *The Meaning of Wilderness*, 48–57.

"The Gremlins of Wind Bay." *Sports Afield*, November 1945.

"Spawning of the Eelpout." *Conservation Volunteer*, January–February 1946.

"We Need Wilderness." *National Parks Magazine*, January–March 1946. Reprinted in condensed form in *Plants and Gardens*, Winter 1946. In *The Meaning of Wilderness*, 58–68.

"On Not Trimming Trees." *Conservation Volunteer*, March–April 1946.

"Canoeing for Sport." *Outdoorsman*, February 1948.

"Let's Finish What We Started." *Outdoor America*, February 1948.

"Moon Magic." *Sports Afield*, February 1948.

"Veterans Named." *Christian Science Monitor*, March 22, 1948.

"Quetico–Superior Elegy." *Living Wilderness*, Spring 1948.

"Quetico–Superior Challenge." *Sports Afield*, May 1948.

"Wings over the Wilderness." *American Forests*, June 1948.

"Voyageur's Return." *Nature Magazine*, June–July 1948.

"The Know-How in Camping." *Outdoorsman*, August 1948.

"The Preservation of Wilderness." *Living Wilderness*, Autumn 1948. In *The Meaning of Wilderness*, 69–78.

"Rainbow Forty." *Star Weekly* (Toronto), October 2, 1948.

"Spawning of the Pike." *Conservation Volunteer*, January–February 1949.

"Battle for a Wilderness." *Forest and Outdoors*, March 1949.

"Frog Chorus." *Conservation Volunteer*, April 1949.

"Canadians Urge International Forest." *Ely (Minn.) Miner*, September 1, 1949.

"Voyageurs' Country." *National Home Monthly*, October 1949.

"Swift as the Wild Goose Flies." *National Parks Magazine*, October–December 1949.

1950s

"A Victory for Wilderness!" *Outdoor America*, January 1950.

"Late Frontier Quetico–Superior." *American Heritage*, Spring 1950.

"Wilderness Victory." *National Parks Magazine*, April–June 1950.

"Airplane Ban Goes into Effect." *Outdoor America*, January–February 1951.

"Canoe Country." *North Country*, Spring 1951.

"The Drummer." *North Country*, Spring 1951.

"Spring Fever." *North Country*, Spring 1951.

"Calling of the Loon." *North Country*, Summer 1951.

"Grand Portage Dedication." *North Country*, Summer 1951.

"Orchids of the North." *North Country*, Summer 1951.

"The Quetico–Superior Wilderness Laboratory." *Science Teacher*, November 1951. In *The Meaning of Wilderness*, 79–83.

"The Rainy Lake Pollution Problem." *Outdoor America*, November–December 1951.

"The Big Snow." *Gopher Historian*, January 1953.

"Voyageur's Country: The Story of the Quetico–Superior Country." *Wilson Bulletin*, March 1953.

"Conservation and Citizenship." *Gopher Historian*, April 1953.

"Airplanes to Wilderness." *Living Wilderness*, Spring 1953.

"Wilderness and the Flambeau." *Living Wilderness*, Spring 1953.

"Let's Take a Canoe Trip." *Recreation*, February 1954.

"The Challenge of Our National Parks." *National Parks Magazine*, April–June 1954.

"The Intangible Values in Nature Protection." *National Parks Magazine*, July–September 1954.

"Canoe Country Manners." *Duluth News Tribune*, September 5, 1954.

"Right Should Prevail." *Outdoor America*, July–August 1955.

"This Is No Little Bird Book." *Living Wilderness*, Winter–Spring 1955–56.

"The Association's First Objective." *National Parks Magazine*, January–March 1956.

"A U.S. Comment." *American Forests*, February 1956.

"The Association's Second Objective." *National Parks Magazine*, April–June 1956.

"The Association's Third Objective." *National Parks Magazine*, July–September 1956.

"The Association's Fourth Objective." *National Parks Magazine*, October–December 1956.

"Outlaw Country." *True*, February 1957.

"Our Need of Breathing Space." In *Perspectives on Conservation*, ed. Henry Jarrett. Baltimore: The Johns Hopkins University Press, 1958. Also in *The Meaning of Wilderness*, 92–99.

"Winning a Wilderness." *Naturalist*, Winter 1958.

"Leisure Time: Man's Key to Self Realization—The Out-of-Doors." *Minnesota Journal of Education*, April 1958.

"The Quetico–Superior." *Outdoor America*, May 1958.

"Thanksgiving: More Than a Holiday." *Outdoor America*, November 1958.

"Of Worms and Fishermen." *Outdoor America*, April 1959.

"Beauty Belongs to All." *Naturalist*, Fall 1959. In *The Meaning of Wilderness*, 100–107.

"Wilderness Manners." *Forest and Outdoors*, October 1959.

"Woodsmen's Skill for the Wild." *Living Wilderness*, Winter 1959–60.

1960S THROUGH 1982

"Winning a Wilderness." *Outdoor America*, June 1960.

"Some New Books in Review: Portage into the Past." *Minnesota History*, March 1961.

"Explorers." *Naturalist*, Winter 1961.

"The Meaning of the National Parks." In *National Parks: A World Need*, ed. Victor H. Cahalane. Special Publication no. 14. New York: American Committee for International Wild Life Protection, 1962.

"The Wilderness Concept." *Ames Forester*, 1962 annual. In *The Meaning of Wilderness*, 122–33.

"Six Decades of Progress." *American Forests*, October 1962.

"Sam Campbell, Philosopher of the Forest." *American Forests*, October 1962.

"Relics from the Rapids." *National Geographic*, September 1963.

"Wilderness Preservation." *Naturalist*, Winter 1964.

"Voyageur's Autumn." *Boys' Life*, November 1964.

"Minnesota's Proposed National Park." *Naturalist*, Spring 1965.

"Skindiving for Treasures of the Past." *Ford Times*, April 1965.

"Natural Resource Readings: A Wilderness Bill of Rights." *Journal of Soil and Water Conservation*, March–April 1966.

"Wilderness Canoe Country: Minnesot'a Greatest Recreational Asset." *Naturalist*, Spring 1967.

"What Is Wilderness?" *Living Wilderness*, Spring 1968. In *The Meaning of Wilderness*, 151–53.

"A Certain Kind of Man." *Beaver*, Autumn 1968.

"A Tribute to F. L. Jaques." *Naturalist*, Spring 1970.

"Wilderness Challenge." *Living Wilderness*, Summer 1970.

"Wilderness Besieged: The Canoe Country of Minnesota." *Audubon*, July 1970.

"The Values of Voyageurs National Park." *Minnesota Conservation Volunteer*, May–June 1971.

"Alaska: Land of Scenic Grandeur." *Living Wilderness*, Winter 1971–72.

"What of Beautiful Minnesota?" In *Century 2: In Perspective*. Minneapolis: Northwestern National Bank, 1972.

"A Longing for Wilderness." In *Wilderness U.S.A.*, ed. Seymour L. Fishbein. Washington, D.C.: National Geographic Society, 1973. In *The Meaning of Wilderness*, 154–73.

"A Giant Step North." *Rotarian*, March 1974.
"Wild Islands of the Shield." *Naturalist*, Summer 1975.
"Caribou Creek." *Audubon*, March 1982.

Speeches Published in Conference Proceedings

"Air Space Reservations over Wilderness." Presented in March 1949, this speech is in *Transactions of the Fourteenth North American Wildlife Conference*. Washington, D.C.: Wildlife Management Institute, 1949.

"Conservation Appeal." Presented in March 1950, this speech is in *Transactions of the Fifteenth North American Wildlife Conference*. Washington, D.C.: Wildlife Management Institute, 1950.

"Summarization of the Sixteenth North American Wildlife Conference." Presented in March 1951, this speech is in *Transactions of the Sixteenth North American Wildlife Conference*. Washington, D.C.: Wildlife Management Institute, 1951.

"Our Public Lands: Shall the Public Abdicate Control?" Presented in March 1958, this speech is in *Transactions of the Twenty-third North American Wildlife Conference*. Washington, D.C.: Wildlife Management Institute, 1958.

"The Spiritual Aspects of Wilderness." Olson gave this talk in April 1961 at the Seventh Biennial Wilderness Conference, held in San Francisco. It is published in David Brower, ed., *Wilderness: America's Living Heritage*. San Francisco: Sierra Club, 1961. In *The Meaning of Wilderness*, 108–21.

"A Philosophical Concept." Olson gave this talk in July 1962 during the First World Conference on National Parks, held in Seattle. It is included in Alexander B. Adams, ed., *First World Conference on National Parks*. Washington, D.C., 1964.

"The Spiritual Need." Olson gave this talk in April 1965 at the Ninth Biennial Wilderness Conference, held in San Francisco. It was published in Bruce M. Kilgore, ed., *Wilderness in a Changing World*. San Francisco: Sierra Club, 1966. In *The Meaning of Wilderness*, 134–44.

"From the Friday Afternoon Discussion." This technically isn't a speech, but there are some interesting comments from Olson in this reprinted discussion that took place during the Tenth Wilderness Conference in San Francisco in April 1967. It is published in Maxine E. McCloskey and James P. Gilligan, ed., *Wilderness and the Quality of Life*. San Francisco: Sierra Club, 1969.

Sigurd F. Olson (1899–1982) was one of the greatest environmentalists of the twentieth century. A conservation activist and popular writer, he introduced a generation of Americans to the importance of wilderness. He served as president of the Wilderness Society and the National Parks Association and was a consultant to the federal government on wilderness preservation and ecological problems. He earned many honors, including the highest recognition possible from the Sierra Club, National Wildlife Federation, and Izaak Walton League.

His books developed a new aesthetic of nature writing that was infused with beauty and respect for our nation's wild places. He received the John Burroughs Medal, the highest award for nature writing, and his works frequently appeared on best-seller lists across the nation.

He lived and worked in Ely, Minnesota, gateway to the Quetico–Superior region, for most of his life.

David Backes is professor of journalism and mass communication at the University of Wisconsin-Milwaukee. His book *A Wilderness Within: The Life of Sigurd F. Olson* (Minnesota, 1997) won the 1998 Small Press Book Award for best biography. He is also the editor of Sigurd F. Olson's *The Meaning of Wilderness: Essential Articles and Speeches* (Minnesota, 2001) and author of *Canoe Country: An Embattled Wilderness* and *The Wilderness Companion*.